W9-AXF-717

ENGLISH SILVER

JACKET ILLUSTRATION

Silver for tea and coffee. The late rococo tea-caddy chased with flowers, shells, scrolls and foliage within asymmetrical panels enclosing chinoiserie designs of tea pickers was by a maker using a mark NH in 1769. The fancy oval teapot of fluted drum form, decorated with bright-cut borders in the neo-classical style, was made in 1788, probably by John Sanders. The early rococo was often relatively restrained, as in this coffee-pot of 1738 (by Peter Archambo) with tucked-in base, the rococo chased scrolls and foliage restricted to the shoulder and base. The scissor tongs, of typical mid-eighteenth century style, were made by John Frost about 1760. (Photographer, Peter Parkinson)

FRONTISPIECE

Bold, large tankard of typical late seventeenth-century style, with reeded rim foot, scroll handle and double scroll thumb-piece and with domed cover: it was made in London in 1688, and the maker's mark is EG between mullets. The small candlestick, by Ebenezer Coker, 1762, presents a challenge for the collector: it is one of a pair numbered 3 and 4 – possibly numbers 1 and 2 still exist. The elegant small jug with beaded decoration and small applied medallions modelled on classical gems is typical of the work of Andrew Fogelburg and Stephen Gilvert, who made it in 1780. The salt on four hoof feet, with shaped gadrooned rim is by Robert Hennell, in a style used extensively in the second half of the eighteenth century. (Photographer, Peter Parkinson)

ENGLISH
SILVER

by
Judith
Banister

HAWTHORN BOOKS, INC.
Publishers · New York

CARL A. RUDISILL LIBRARY
LENOIR RHYNE COLLEGE

739.237
B22e
62375
August, 1968

© Judith Banister, 1965. Copyright under International and Pan-American Copyright Conventions. All rights reserved, including the right to reproduce this book, or portions thereof, in any form, except for the inclusion of brief quotations in a review. All inquiries should be addressed to Hawthorn Books, Inc., 70 Fifth Avenue, New York City 10011. Library of Congress Catalogue Card Number: 66–16161.

First American Edition, 1966

Printed in Great Britain

3430

CONTENTS

ACKNOWLEDGEMENTS

The author is indebted to the following for the use of illustrative material in this book. (Numbers in **bold face** refer to plates.)

Ashmolean Museum **39, 41, 44, 59, 65, 72, 75, 78, 80, 83, 84, 87**. Barber Institute of Fine Art, Birmingham **4**: Biggs of Maidenhead Ltd. **30, 74**. Birmingham Museum and Art Gallery **67**. Bracher & Sydenham Ltd. **89, 98**; **27, 37, 56, 57, 81, 86, 92, 94, 101, 103, 122**. Bruford & Son Ltd. **29, 49**. Christie, Manson & Woods Ltd. **5, 8, 15, 20, 24, 33, 43, 47, 51, 52, 88, 96, 100, 102, 109, 111, 121, 125, 126**. Garrard & Co. Ltd. **14, 28, 79**. A. B. Gilbert Ltd. **55**. P.C. Gray Esq. **1, 25**. Hereford Corporation **16**. N. C. Hurst Esq. **21**. Ideal Home Magazine **47, 57, 60** (photographer, Colin Tait). Ironmongers Company **21**. Thomas Lumley Ltd. **35**; **54, 62, 68, 71, 116, 120, 123, 124**. Melbourne Art Gallery, Felton Bequest **9**. The Minneapolis Museum of Arts **25**; **73**. Mrs W. B. Munro **7, 17, 26, 98**. G. S. Sanders Esq. jacket and frontispiece, **93, 95**; **2, 11, 19, 36**, S. J. Shrubsole Ltd. **35, 42, 45, 46, 50, 66, 85, 90, 93, 112**. Sotheby & Co. Ltd. **10, 53, 99, 110**. Spink & Son Ltd. **89**. Sterling & Francine Clark Art Institute, Williamstown, Massachusetts **40, 69, 76, 91, 95, 108**. Temple Newsam House, Leeds **12, 32**. Toledo Museum of Art, Ohio (Gift of Florence Scott Libbey) **77**. Judge Irwin Untermeyer **18**. C. J. Vander Ltd. **128**. Victoria & Albert Museum **11, 30, 38**; **12, 34, 48, 58, 118, 131**. Walter H. Willson Ltd. **25, 38, 60, 61, 64, 104, 105, 106, 107, 113, 114**. Worshipful Company of Goldsmiths **15, 60, 78, 79, 80, 82, 85**; **3, 13, 22, 79, 82, 119, 127, 132, 134, 135**.

The author and publishers are indebted to the following for reference and permission to reproduce assay marks appearing on pages 68 to 77: *Hall-Marks on Plate*, W. Chaffers (5th edition, 1875); Frederick Bradbury Publications Ltd, *Guide to Marks of Origin on British and Irish Silver Plate from Mid 16th Century to the year 1963 and old Sheffield Plate Makers' Marks 1743-1860* (11th edition); *English Goldsmiths and their Marks* (2nd edition 1921, reprinted 1949), Sir Charles Jackson.

INTRODUCTION

Because silver is in itself a beautiful metal that loses nothing by being left plain and may gain a great deal by judicious decoration, appreciation comes easily. The splendours of a Queen Anne ewer, the graceful curves of a coffee-pot, the charm of a patch box or the massive co-ordination of a ceremonial centre-piece all have their place in the story of silver. Almost always it is a place assured also by a date, the place of making and the name of the craftsman. Even unmarked silver can usually be dated to within a few years – to the extent perhaps of being given a maker – for the development of silver styles over the centuries was slow, and changes when they came were usually definite.

It is these qualities – beauty and the easily-traced progression of silver styles – that makes the appeal of silver so insidious. For silver attracts with its appearance and its feel, and then plunges the admirer into a lifetime of most absorbing study.

The first impact of silver may be apparently insignificant – the chance examination of the small marks on a Christening cup or an inherited tea service. The initial appeal of a piece is visual, but almost immediately there is an awareness that the hallmarks mean something – when, where, by whom was it made? How does the piece reflect its period, is it typical or unusual? Try to answer but one of these questions, and silver, old or new, is applying its own special charm.

The study of silver is an enormous subject, but never a dull one. It reaches back into the era of prehistory, it has left its trail in every country and in every age. Over the years much silver has been lost, but students of English silver are fortunate that no real devastation has been suffered since the Civil War. Since then, English silver has seen its richest and most exciting periods. The craft has been refreshed by new and vigorous blood from abroad, and wealth at home has meant plenty, not only for the very rich but for the moderately well-to-do middle classes as well.

Some sixty-five years ago, however, Ruskin castigated people's attitude to silver, their revolt against their ancestral plate and their sending everything to be melted down "and made up with new flourishes and fresh lustre". "The way to have a truly noble service of plate," he went on, "is to keep adding to it, not melting it." Today, at least, we are fostering a new appreciation of the skill of the silversmith. It is a slow, long process, but Ruskin can rest at ease. There is no shortage of silver enthusiasts today, though the more there are, the greater the chances that our young craftsmen will learn from, and develop, the fine tradition of English silversmithing.

I

THE TRADITIONS OF ENGLISH DOMESTIC SILVER

The paradox of English silver design is that the results are so very English. Since mediaeval times English silversmiths have rarely innovated, but have eagerly assimilated the styles and manners of Continental designers. Yet English silver is almost always unmistakably English and, to the collector, incomparable with the silver of any other craftsmen in any other country.

This ability to make alien styles their own is not confined to the silversmiths of London. It is equally true of the provincial, Scottish and Irish silversmiths. Scottish silver has many distinctive qualities, and Irish silver, which in the eighteenth century in particular was of exceptionally high quality and vied with that of London, often betrays itself as Irish without so much as a glance at the hallmark.

By far the greatest quantity of English silver was made in London, although there are long and strong traditions of crafts-manship in other parts of the country. Exeter, Chester, Newcastle, York and many other towns were centres of silversmithing for many centuries. Now, of the provincial assay offices where silver has to be tested and marked, only Birmingham and Sheffield, both set up in 1773, are left outside London. In Scotland, Edinburgh is the sole surviving office, while Dublin assays and marks the silver made in Eire.

As the centre of commerce and culture, London has always attracted wealth, and where there is wealth there are goldsmiths and silversmiths. During the seventeenth century wealthy gold-smiths often concerned themselves with usury and with banking, and even during the eighteenth century not a few silversmiths advertised that they kept 'running cashes'. This was, in fact, quite a logical situation. Gold and silver were, in effect, so much bullion that happened to be on hand in a pleasant and useful form. The goldsmiths, not unexpectedly, held reserves of gold – especially after the Mint no longer afforded them security during the Civil War. Thus it was only a small step to becoming a banker – like Sheriff Meynell, whom Pepys described as "the great money man" and who made a fortune out of lending money at fifteen, or even twenty, per cent. Many a fortune was lost, however, in 1672 when Charles II closed the Exchequer, and from then onwards, though still often called goldsmiths, the bankers began to become specialists in financial affairs rather than workers in silver and gold.

The patron of the silversmith still tended to look on his plate as a sort of public bank-balance. The more he had on show about the house, the more he was esteemed as a wealthy man. If he needed money, he melted down some of his plate. After all, it was of the same sterling standard as the coinage, so conversion was simple enough. In the same way, if he grew tired of the design of his silver (often known as *white plate*) or his silver-gilt (carelessly dubbed *gold* or *gilt*), then he just had it remade in the current fashion. There were no connoisseurs or collectors as such; they were a nineteenth century phenomenon as far as silver was concerned. The only sort of collecting was the accumulation of wealth.

The Restoration of Charles II in 1660 is usually considered the beginning of the era of domestic silver. Before that, it is not easy to trace the evolution of silver design in any great detail. The Church during the Middle Ages had been the patron of the arts – Saint Dunstan, the patron Saint of goldsmiths, was himself a gold-smith – but the ravages of the Reformation had taken a heavy toll

A baroque engraving of silversmiths at work from a book of designs by M. Mouton of Lyon, now in the Victoria and Albert Museum.

▶

VIGILAT ET CVSTODIT

ANGVLI

LIVRE
DE
DESSEINS
POUR
Toute Sorte d'ouvrages
d'Orfévrerie et ornements
propres à plusieurs sortes d'arts
Inuenté et Gravé par le
Sr. Mr. Mouton Orfeure
a Lyon natif de mons en
hainault

INRI

of mediaeval treasures. Added to that there had been the heavy demands of war over the centuries, the lavish gifts made to foreign potentates and, finally, the wholesale destruction of plate to support one side or the other during the Civil War – quite apart from wear and tear and the common habit of melting plate to have it refashioned. Indeed, until the Elizabethan period it is almost impossible to make a proper assessment of the progress of styles, and even then records and relics are scanty, the latter being consequently expensive. For the collector pre-Restoration silver, even small articles such as spoons, beakers, tumbler cups and wine tasters, is often beyond reach. This is not to suggest that silver of the mediaeval, Tudor and early Stuart periods should be ignored. The museums and the textbooks, perhaps naturally enough since most pre-Restoration pieces are truly 'museum pieces', usually put special emphasis on the surviving treasures, many of which are very fine indeed. The Renaissance, which came late to England and did not make much impact on silver until the 1530's, was the source of all European design tradition for centuries to come. Its decoration, based on revived classicism, with flutes and acanthus leafage, swags of fruit, flowers and scrolls, satisfied the appetite of artists virtually until the mid-eighteenth century when its themes became out of hand, and it needed Adam and the neo-classicists to formalise its motifs by returning to the ancient originals once more.

The influences on English silver, from Holbein at the court of Henry VIII to that of Van Vianen at Charles I's court, were always European. Foreign silversmiths working in London and elsewhere were no phenomenon, though most must have returned hastily to their own countries at the time of the Civil War. There was during and immediately after the Civil War a break in the history of the craft. For more than a decade before the return of Charles II the trade, in London at any rate, was virtually in abeyance. A few pieces were made, occasionally well, but often flimsily and with rather immature decoration. Few apprentices were trained, and there was a dearth of silver as well as of money to pay for it. The Commonwealth government did not encourage spending on luxury goods.

The Restoration betokened a new England in more ways than one. It coincided with new developments in science and industry, art and architecture, trade and overseas enterprise. There was plenty to be done, and life was busy. Those who had joined the royal family in exile returned and set about rebuilding their houses, farming the new estates assigned to loyal supporters by the grateful king, and replenishing their stores of plate. Houses and furnishings, if rather chilly and bare by centrally-heated, twentieth-century standards, were much more comfortable and homely than they had been at the beginning of the century. There were the large and prosperous middle classes, all quite prepared to emulate their wealthier neighbours and to buy luxuries whenever they could afford them; and the rich were often very rich indeed. For the silversmith, the return of the king in May, 1660, was the beginning of a long era of work and prosperity. With trade at its lowest ebb, there were problems, but the craft promptly celebrated the occasion by deciding to change the annual date-letter (struck on all plate) from the traditional May 19th, St. Dunstan's Day, to May 29th, the King's birthday.

In contrast to the generally ascetic taste of the Commonwealth period, came an upsurge of demand for bold and showy silver and silver-gilt. There had been prophecy of this in the few cups, beakers, tankards and dishes made during the last years of the Commonwealth. As usual, the impetus came from abroad, and now, the returning court brought new styles home with them. Both France and Holland wielded great influence on silver design. Louis XIV was still a young man, but his famous "L'état, c'est moi" was a dictum already five years old. The French Court in the 1660's was already attracting artists and craftsmen and soaring towards the sun-king splendour of Versailles. In Holland, there was the impact of the floral baroque. The swirled and lobed style of Van Vianen gave way to exuberant flowers and foliage, birds and animals – still bold, still with the emphasis on embossing and chasing, but reflecting the Dutch interest in natural history. Instead of lobed meanderings, great flowers, especially tulips, among which little naked cupids gambolled, covered every inch of the surface. It was a style that appealed enormously to the English gentry and nobility, especially now that everything that could possibly be made in silver, from patch boxes to firedogs, was being hammered out in the busy workshops.

The two-handled cups, variously called porringers, caudle cups and posset cups, are probably the most typical of all Charles II silverwares. Posset and caudle were both spiced milk drinks, curdled with wine or ale and taken hot, so that handled cups were very necessary. The rather squat bulging bodies of these cups were usually embossed and chased with flowers, foliage and animals. A lion on one side and a unicorn on the other – sometimes varied by bears, hounds, deer, boars, goats and the like coursing round the sides amid the foliage – were popular motifs, the bold style of the embossing serving to conceal the rather thin metal. Silver remained in short supply, and demand was heavy, and did not wane. A typical feature of the bulging-bodied porringers was the cast caryatid handles, which became progressively more spindly and more formalised, so that some appear as slender, double scrolls with leafy blobs for heads instead of curvaceous maidens. But they all succeeded in satisfying the demand for richness and suited the wealthy, though not always very tasteful, patrons who were keeping the silversmiths busy. And being busy, the craftsmen soon improved their techniques.

Standing cups, which had been lost in large quantities during the Civil War, were made again, sometimes in styles that harked

A silversmith's workshop in 1707, from an invitation
card issued by the Wardens of the Worshipful
Company of Goldsmiths.

back to the originals that had been melted down. Occasionally, replicas of the great standing salts were made – mostly in the capstan shape on a circular or square base with a waisted spool support for the salt, and with scrolls which presumably held a napkin to keep the salt covered. But the days of the high table were virtually over, except for banquets and great ceremonial occasions, so that silver for show was more likely to be in the form of garnitures for the mantelpiece or fireplace – vases and jars with no other purpose but to gleam and look splendid in firelight and candlelight. Between ten and fifteen inches high, they are typically enriched with floral and foliate embossing enclosing cherubs or masks and with richly festooned applied work round the necks.

Equally richly ornamented were the silver sconces for one or two candles, with shaped oval backplates, and the impressive toilet services with perhaps a dozen or sixteen pieces, including mirror, jewel caskets, pin cushion, flasks, flagons and dishes and even covered bowls elaborately chased with scrolls, leafage and *amorini* in high relief. At Windsor and at Knole is some of the rare furniture of the period, including a table made by Andrew Moore for William III, while candlestick stands and andirons, or firedogs, have occasionally survived. At Ham House, there is a silver fender and a silver bellows, while the most magnificent of all silver furniture must have been the silver bed made in 1676 for Nell Gwynn, perhaps in the style of the silver bed on which Rembrandt had painted his Danäe in 1636.

Not all Charles II silver was rich and gaudy. There had been a leavening in the French style of cut-card work introduced about 1650, for every age of English silver seems to have its adherents of simplicity. Cut-card ornament, consisting of thin silhouettes of silver soldered round the bases of bowls and cups, and round finials and handle sockets, was an effective way of helping to strengthen thin-gauge metal. Its simplicity of outline – at this period the motifs were chiefly simple foliate silhouettes –

appealed to those whose tastes did not assent to the more lavish Dutch styles. Some silver, notably tankards, wine cups and the heavy-based small tumbler cups, on the whole escaped the current passion for overall decoration, other than perhaps a band of acanthus leaf chasing or an engraved coat-of-arms in a plumed mantling.

This porringer and cover with embossed and repoussé-chased acanthus leaf decoration dates from about 1675 and bears only the maker's mark.

Beer was drunk in enormous quantities – even a small family would consume several gallons a week – and tankards were proportionately large. In the Commonwealth period, a spreading base, aptly called a skirt foot, replaced the so-called 'Puritan' type with its base in one with the body and without a foot. By 1660, the rim foot and a slightly tapering cylindrical barrel established the type of tankard that was to be little changed for more than half a century. Unlike the handles on bowls and cups, tankard handles were broad scrolls, sometimes with hoof-like terminals, and with a cast, bifurcated or two-lobed thumbpiece. Tankards were almost always covered, the lid being a flat-domed cap with a small wavy or pointed peak at the front. Base and lip were usually simply moulded or reeded. Incidentally, the small holes found at the base of the scroll handles, sometimes shaped rather like the mouthpiece of a wind instrument, were simply blowholes to allow the air to escape when the handle was soldered on. The fact that some can produce a whistling sound has nothing to do with calling the potboy!

Wine cups, soon to be ousted by glasses, which had become a commercial proposition with Ravenscroft's development of flint glass, were also of the styles most copied in glass. They had a trumpet-shaped bowl and simple baluster stem on a circular moulded foot. Following a really old-established tradition were the small beakers, made in various sizes from about two and a half to seven inches high. They had cylindrical bodies flaring to the rims, and might be plain or decorative as taste and money dictated. Another commonplace in silver was the delightful little tumbler cups which were probably used for spirits or other strong liquors. Rarely more than a couple of inches high, they are heavy-based so that they return to upright even if tilted. Tumbler cups continued to be made throughout the country well into the eighteenth century, and were even made in gold as race prizes at Chester until the 1790's.

After ten years or so the ebullient and flowery Dutch styles were beginning to pall, perhaps because the English silversmiths had not fully mastered the skills needed to create such decorative wares, perhaps because there has always been a taste in England for less showy pieces. At all events, about 1670, several new styles made their appearance in England, though of them only acanthus leafage and fluted baroque (also of Dutch derivation) survived to the end of the century, given new impetus with the arrival of Dutch William on the throne of England.

The baroque was really a formalising of the Dutch naturalistic style. The emphasis was still on embossing and chasing, but had become more restrained. Alternating palm and acanthus leaf chasing was arranged around the bases of cups and tankards, or round the broad rims of dishes. Fluting, both straight and swirled, was similarly used on the lower parts of drinking vessels, and it was a style admirably suited to the column candlesticks of the period, which gradually became plainer until ousted by the cast baluster candlestick in the 1680's.

One unusual and rather rare style used for display plate was to make a tankard or cup quite plain, gild it and then sheathe it with a pierced and chased sleeve, letting the gilded plate beneath gleam through the pierced foliage and flowers, animals, birds and amorini. It is a style of undiscovered origin, though was perhaps derived from Austria or Italy, where serpentine, rock crystal and other minerals were often mounted as cups, bowls and tankards in elaborately worked silver and silver-gilt.

Little is known of what happened to the silversmiths of London during the Commonwealth. Some perhaps may have followed Continental practice and actually travelled abroad, working as journeymen. That may account for the occasional Scandinavian and German baroque styles that made their appearance during the late Charles II period. These were mostly concerned with drinking vessels and their decoration. Beakers and tankards were matted, giving a granulated effect in broad bands that left the foot and lip plain. The almost straight-sided Scandinavian type of barrel came into favour for the tankard, with corded ribs at the base, an inch or so above the foot, and round the cover. Three cast feet, usually in the form of a lion couchant or pomegranates, and with a matching, cast thumbpiece, were often a feature of this imported style. The detail of these castings was often very fine, and they came to be used for thumbpieces on the more traditionally English style of tankard as well. Two very exceptional tankards of 1671 and 1675, both by a maker using a punch with the initials I.H., have this Continental style of barrel with corded ribs and three feet and thumbpiece cast as perched eagles. What is most unusual, however, is the abandoning of the usual scroll handle for one cast in the form of grotesque sea monsters. The earlier of the two, known from its inscriptions as the Dodding Tankard, also exemplifies another of the styles that came into fashion about 1670 – the barrel and cover are engraved with figures and scenes in the style known as *chinoiserie*.

Chinoiserie, or decoration in the Chinese taste, has been a recurrent style in the history of English silver. Its earliest manifestation, from about 1675 to 1690, appears to have been one of the few entirely English decorative inventions. Achieved by either flat-chasing or engraving, chinoiserie was the armchair traveller's idea of the mystic orient. Lightly sketched and rather inaccurate palm trees, spiky foliage, and flowers provided a setting for warriors in short tunics or sages in flowing kimonos, for temples and pavilions, for exotic birds and butterflies. Cups, porringers, tankards, bowls, salvers, jars, vases and complete toilet sets were treated to this rather naïve ornament which was without doubt the homespun conception, inspired by travellers' tales, of the strange lands that were sending spices, silks and "a China drink", called tea, to England.

Tea, coffee and chocolate, all of which were introduced to England about the middle of the century, quickly became fashionable. Coffee and chocolate houses were centres of gossip, business and politics, while tea, though exorbitantly expensive,

Silver for Coffee and Chocolate

nonetheless soon became equally popular. Fashionable beverages needed silverwares from which they could be served. The silversmith's reaction was to adapt the tall flagon, making a tall, tapering, cylindrical pot with a spout and handle. It was a practical and acceptable form that soon established itself as the universal style for both coffee and chocolate, the only difference between the pots for the two drinks being the provision of a small hinged lid within the cover of the chocolate-pot through which the stirrer rod could be inserted.

The baluster or pear shape dominated early eighteenth century domestic silver design. This fine large chocolate pot was made by Alice Sheene in 1706. It is $11\frac{1}{2}$ inches high, on circular-moulded foot, the wood scroll handle set at right angles to the curved spout, the cover with small hinged lid for inserting the stirrer rod to froth the chocolate, and with double-scroll thumb-piece. The pot bears the Iron-mongers' arms and is inscribed "The united gift of Messrs. Simon Owen and Christop. Cletherow".

Early Teapots

The earliest known teapot, dated 1670 and inscribed to the effect that it is indeed a teapot, is in fact identical with the typical coffee-pots. It seems to have been an exception, however, and most of the earliest surviving teapots resemble small Chinese winepots, perhaps derived from porcelain or stoneware originals. The earliest of these little pots is unmarked, but on evidence of the arms of Archbishop Sharp which it bears, it must be dated before his death in 1679. It is small, pear-shaped without being waisted, the cover forming the narrowing part in line with the body. A small S-shaped spout, set close to the body, and a handle opposite the spout are provided on this and on two other similar, but later, teapots, one in the Ashmolean Museum, the other in the Victoria & Albert Museum. Both were made about 1690.

Increased colonisation and trade with both east and west brought many other products within the reach of a growing population at home. The second half of the seventeenth century saw a large rise in the consumption of both sugar and spices, and the first casters in silver date from the reign of Charles II. Here again, the straight-sided cylinder provided the basic style, with a high-domed, pierced cover held in place by sturdy bayonet clamps. Like most of the straight-sided wares of the silversmith, casters called for little decoration, and ornament was chiefly restricted to piercing, a shallow band of fluting or acanthus chasing, cut-card work or engraving.

Perhaps it was the prosperous state of life in England that made the persecuted craftsmen of France turn to this country when Louis XIV revoked the Edict of Nantes in 1685. For some years less and less toleration had been afforded to the Protestants in France, and many Huguenots did not wait for the final blow in 1685 before they fled to friendlier countries, chiefly Flanders, England, Germany and America. The Revocation merely increased the flow, turning a small stream into a torrent. Many of the Huguenots were craftsmen, silversmiths among them.

London and its prosperity must have seemed a haven of peace and plenty, though for the refugees, trying to find homes and work with no more than the tools in their hands to support them, life was far from simple. The London silversmiths did not take kindly to a large number of foreigners in their midst. Despite Royal and other appeals, made even before 1685, many skilled Huguenot silversmiths found themselves struggling as mere journeymen for London masters – if they managed to find work at all.

In 1682, Pierre Harache, an exceptionally fine craftsman – "lately come from France for to avoid persecution and live quietly" – managed to break down the trade's resistance and obtained his Freedom of the Goldsmiths' Company. His was as yet a rare case of success, but he and his fellow Frenchmen, most of them from the provinces, were soon exerting a tremendous influence on English silversmithing and laying the foundation for the supremacy of English silver during the coming century. Harache's own work shows the essential appreciation of detail and design that typifies the best of Huguenot work. It was a consummately skilful combination of simplicity of line and ordered, imaginative decoration. The Huguenot style appealed to even the most vociferous of the protesting London goldsmiths, who adopted it eagerly and no doubt gladly employed the crafts-men who had the ability to do such work, even while they were petitioning and doing all they could to prevent the Huguenots from setting up workshops on their own account.

The Huguenots had a tremendous contribution to make to English silversmithing. Since most of them came from the provinces, they were not so subject to the impulsive whim of fashion as those who worked in Paris for the French aristocracy. Their tradition was one of fine craftsmanship, sturdy gauge silver and meticulous decorative detail. They brought with them, no doubt, the design books they used in their native towns of Metz, Rouen, Poitou and so on – design books that

23

laid emphasis on the detailed ornament known in France as *Régence* – ordered arrangements of strapwork enclosing scrolls, shells, husks and foliage, of applied lion and human head masks, of delicate cut-card and other applied work. They also brought a new variety of forms, based chiefly on the baluster shape. They introduced the cast baluster candlestick and ousted the fluted column type; they turned the straight-sided flagon into a graceful ewer with a broad high lip and flying scroll handle; they heightened the two-handled cup, making it well-proportioned and elegant with a moulded rib round the body together with a sturdy scroll or harp-shaped handles, thus ridding the silversmiths' shelves for good and all of bulging-bodied cups and coarse and ungainly embossing. Formality, simple curves and detail of design and decoration were the keynotes of Huguenot work. It was a harnessing and a control of all the themes of the silversmith; a riot of acanthus leaves and swirling foliage became a neat repetitive border or a series of flowerheads and palm leaves; swirls became formal flutes, unbridled nursery animals were turned into small neat lion masks.

The English silversmiths were quite prepared to accept the new simplicity, which they had already used themselves for drinking vessels and footed salvers. From the time of the great influx of Huguenot craftsmen, however, two distinct styles emerged – one continuing the traditions of English baroque, the other of definitely French inspiration. At times, the two merged. Silver for coffee, for instance, largely remained in the English tradition, the straight-sided, cylindrical pot with a curved spout at right angles to the scroll handle being accepted as the general style by all the silversmiths. Established, too, was the baluster cast candlestick (though the earliest ones were in fact the work of Pierre Harache in the early 1680's); with moulded, octagonal bases with sunk centres and knopped stems with cylindrical sockets, they set the style for the next half-century.

The English silversmiths seem to have remained the chief

makers of some wares – perhaps understandably, since the use of
silver for beer and punch drinking was typically English. Tankards remained plain and capacious; punch bowls and wine glass
coolers were relics of the baroque, with fluted and gadroon-
bordered panels and scalloped rims chased with cherub masks,
scrolls and acanthus foliage in the most honoured baroque
tradition. But when patrons wanted presentation cups and
covers, dishes or ewers, they tended to approach the Huguenot
designers for their French styles that were, in fact, slowly
permeating the English silversmiths' workshops as well.

While the London goldsmiths and the newly arrived Huguenots
battled for custom, the Government was beginning to take a
none too benevolent interest in the craft. So great was the
demand for silverwares that not a few silversmiths were
apparently using the coinage of the realm to make plate. In
March, 1697, the Act "for encouraging the bringing in of
wrought plate to be coined" reversed the process. In addition,
all new wrought silver had to be of a higher standard of fineness
than sterling, which had been in force since 1300. This higher
standard silver, containing 3.3 per cent more silver, was known
as the *Britannia Standard*, because the plate had to be marked by
the assay offices with a punch showing "the figure of a woman
commonly called Britannia".

The period of Britannia silver lasted from March, 1697, until
June, 1720. It covers some of the most prolific and finest years
of English silver. Silver of this period was frequently quite plain,
relying for its appeal on the beauty of line and the soft reflected
mouldings. This plainness has, however, nothing to do with the
use of the softer, high-standard silver, as has been suggested by
some writers. Britannia takes decoration very well and in skilled
hands even better than sterling. It was merely a coincidence
that much silver of the period was plain. Indeed, even after 1720
when the higher standard was no longer obligatory Paul De
Lamerie, acclaimed justly as one of the greatest of all silversmiths,

continued to use it for another twelve years, not even troubling to register a mark for sterling until 1732. Any implication in the wording of the Act of 1719, which restored the old sterling standard, that the new standard was too soft was probably due to the silversmiths' desire to be allowed to use the less costly sterling. Certainly, no one has ever had to complain that Britannia silver, of which large quantities are still in daily use, does not stand up to wear. Restoration of sterling, however, had a typical government sting in its tail – it was to bear a duty of sixpence per ounce.

Paul De Lamerie had a supreme feeling for design and decoration, and produced many superbly ornamented pieces at a time when most work was relatively plain. One of his most magnificent pieces of all is this wine cistern of 1719 from the collection of the Duke of Sutherland and now in The Minneapolis Institute of Arts. The cistern is oval, 38 inches long by 18 inches wide, and stands on a high oval foot richly repoussé with strapwork, husks and rosettes on a scalework ground below a band of shells and foliate scrolls on a matted ground. The bowl is convex, plain at the base except for later engraved arms, but rising to a matted band enriched with eight grotesque masks and shells alternating among strapwork. At the centre on either side is a huge bearded mask.

The Baluster Form

In the early years of the Britannia period, coinciding with the reign of Queen Anne, the Huguenot styles gradually gained an ascendancy over the native ones. Probably patrons found the French designs to their liking, and the English silversmiths had perforce to follow suit. Possibly the new styles appealed also to the finer silversmiths of London, men more skilled than their fathers and grandfathers who had been beset by political and economic unrest. Changes in silver design are always slow. Perhaps the long years of apprenticeship may be a cause. A man learns his craft from an established master over seven long years. By the time he is a master silversmith himself, he has probably developed his own style, and is able to offer that to his own patrons and to pass it on to his own apprentices. In the close-knit communities of the seventeenth and eighteenth centuries there was less insistence on change for its own sake. Changes came deliberately and definitely, but often they were really only changes in detail, developing always out of a previous form. Only on rare occasions – as the great Huguenot influx – did the progress of silver design leap forward instead of marching along at an easy pace.

The baluster form soon dominated most silverwares. Casters, candlesticks, jugs and teapots showed gracious curves. Coffee-pots, though mostly straight-sided, conformed with curving swan-necked spouts and scroll handles. Even some mugs and tankards appeared with tucked-in base on a circular moulded foot. The teapot of the Queen Anne period had grown away from the wine-pot style into a squat pear shape, with a high-domed cover and curved spout. Following suit was an addition to the tea-table – the tea-kettle, provided with a baluster-legged stand with a spirit lamp or charcoal brazier beneath. Only the tea-caddy stayed firmly unaffected by the baluster curve, remaining an oblong or octagonal canister, usually with a bottle-like top and sliding base. Perhaps because chocolate was more fashionable in France than in England, French styles of baluster chocolate-pot were made, usually by immigrant silversmiths, in early eighteenth-century London. A few were even so French as to have straight turned-wood handles instead of D-shapes or scrolls, and flat cap covers instead of the high-domed ones that were usual.

Entirely French in conception, and almost always made by French silversmiths in England, were helmet-shaped jugs and ewers. Differing considerably in decorative detail, they were generally of similar form; mounted on a circular, moulded foot, the body was divided by two ribs; the upper one followed the outline of the rim and spout and usually featured an applied mask or other decoration immediately below the spout; the flying-scroll handle was sometimes cast as an arching caryatid. The bases were usually, though not invariably, enriched with applied work.

Applied detail and engraving were the two great decorative treatments of the Queen Anne period. Though much domestic silver was relatively plain, few important 'state' pieces were left unadorned, and both Huguenot and native silversmiths achieved some splendid pieces which demonstrated their fine command of ornament. At the turn of the century there was a revival and a refinement of cut-card ornament, particularly by Harache and his countryman, David Willaume. Delicate and detailed cut-out designs, sometimes enhanced with chasing, were applied round the bases of cups, ewers, bowls, pilgrim flasks (the great wine bottles used for cooling wine), coffee-pots, teapots, tankards and jugs. The tops of casters were often ornamented with cut-card; one unusual set included a caster with the cards having the details of the leafage unpierced – perhaps to differentiate between one spice and another.

Cast applied detail was another Huguenot trait soon adopted by all competent silversmiths. The use of cast thumbpieces and finials was extended to applied details below the spouts of jugs and ewers, to lion and human mask handles on punch bowls and wine cisterns, and to tiny lion masks applied at the shoulders of cast baluster candlesticks. Cast applied strapwork, palm leaf and lambrequin ornament became more elaborate and detailed, especially on the cups and covers, wine pails and wine fountains ordered by the now extremely wealthy families who patronised the London silversmiths.

Engraving on silver was of an exceptionally high order during the reigns of William III, Queen Anne and George I, and a number of very beautiful salvers and dishes – mostly made during the high-standard period – have survived. In contrast, some salvers and waiters were completely plain, or decorated no more than with a moulded or gadrooned rim and an engraved coat-of-arms or crest. Variety was sometimes achieved by the form only – square, circular, octagonal, hexagonal or multi-lobed. Shallow dishes with fluted edges, known as strawberry dishes, were made in various sizes from small saucer types to large bowls, some nine or ten inches in diameter. These, too, might be left plain, or delicately chased or engraved within each of the flutes.

The reign of George I saw the new age of the dining service. Plates and dishes in silver were nothing new, but now there were also soup tureens, sauce boats, and knives, forks and spoons made *en suite*. Forks in England had been rather late arrivals (those made prior to 1690 being very rare indeed), and according to Fanny Burney, as recently as the end of the eighteenth century they were not exactly plentiful – even in the royal household. They were, however, included among the dinner-table wares of the early eighteenth-century home, and guests were no longer expected to bring their own with them. About the turn of the seventeenth century, the trifid end of spoons and forks became rounded off to the shield top, with a flattened stem and a rat-tail down the back of the spoon-bowl. Forks were sometimes two-pronged, usually three-pronged. During the reign of Queen Anne, the shield top was replaced by the round end, known as Hanoverian, but still with a plain rat-tail. Hanoverian remained

The Rococo

the favourite pattern of flatware until superseded by Old English in the later eighteenth century and by more decorative patterns during the Regency.

The change back to sterling had little effect on silver design. Plain moulded ribs, gadrooning and scroll handles were well suited to the heavy gauge metal used by most silversmiths. For the wealthy, decorative detail of great intricacy could be achieved by using applied cast and pierced ornament and flat chasing, which was now more frequently employed. But the use of ornament was growing, and even as early as 1722 silversmiths of the calibre of Paul De Lamerie were making wider use of elaborate cast and chased applied cartouches and other details. Within a decade or so, the decorative style began to predominate. It was but a small step to the most decorative of all decoration – the rococo.

Rococo was of French origin. In France it had been accepted nearly a quarter of a century earlier than in England, and indeed had almost run out its time there before it found a foothold here. It probably takes its strange name from *rocaille*, and was, indeed, a fantasy of rocks and marine creatures, flowers and shells and scrolls, leaping dolphins and foliate fronds. It expressed movement by using asymmetry, and most successfully catered for the rich man's desire to own something out of the ordinary, something quite distinct from the formality and simplicity of the previous twenty-five years.

This superb silver-gilt cup, made by Thomas Heming in 1759 and given to the Victoria and Albert Museum by the Esso Petroleum Company, was one of the last essays in the riotous rococo style, soon to be ousted by the simplicity of neo-classicism; $16\frac{1}{2}$ inches high, the vase-shaped body is swirl-fluted and applied with vine leaves and tendrils, caterpillars, snails and other insects—all beautifully modelled. Thomas Heming was Royal Goldsmith in the time between 1761 and 1783.

▶

The rococo turned formality upside down. Even the simple, pear shape of the teapot and kettle was inverted so that the shoulders could provide a better and broader surface for more decoration. The baluster stem of the candlestick swirled to one side, swelling as it spread upwards, or it was changed into a draped figure which upheld the sconce. The base, like the sides of kettles and casters, tea-caddies and tureens, sauce boats and cake baskets, would be a rockery of shells and flowers, snails and scrolls, twisting and turning as they carried the asymmetrical design to the top of the piece.

The rococo demanded all the silversmith's skills, with casting and chasing predominating to achieve richness of decoration. Applied cast and chased borders for salvers, waiters, trays and table baskets were further elaborated by piercing and sometimes by engraved and flat chased detail as well.

About 1750 there was another revival of chinoiserie, this time executed in repoussé chased designs and in pierced work. It was an aptly popular fashion for all kinds of tea-table silver. Many a caddy and sugar-box was chased with robed figures, oriental flowers and gabled houses in the Chinese taste. As often as not, the chinoiserie designs were inextricably mixed with the scrolls and shells of the rococo to create exotic and extravagant tributes to the cult of tea-drinking. Tea and China also contributed inspiration for the rare tea-chest caddies, their box-like sides adorned with Chinese symbols – not always entirely appropriate ones – and their covers mounted with finials in the form of tea-plants.

During the 1760's pagoda-like roofs, Chinese figures and temple bells appeared on the elaborately pierced basket épergnes used as table centrepieces on formal occasions. The bridges, coolie figures, palm trees and strange plants associated by the English silversmiths with Chinese art were used with considerable delicacy for the pierced baskets and épergne stands as a contrast to the cherub-mounted, scrolling branches and shell-

and flower-crusted rococo épergnes. Even pierced salts with cut-glass bowls were made about 1760 by Emick Romer, a Norwegian silversmith working in London who appears to have specialised in épergnes and baskets. Another specialist maker of épergnes was Thomas Pitts of Ayr Street, Piccadilly, where later the famous Paul Storr was also to have a workshop.

The extreme fantasy of the rococo with its turbulent movement and cloying multiplicity of confused metaphors was too much for some patrons, even at the height of its fashion. Indeed, throughout the 1740's and 1750's there had always been a steady demand for silver in what could almost be termed a decorative baroque style. The shells, lion masks and applied scrolls were those of the rococoists, but they were often used with formality and symmetry, especially for sauce boats, baluster-shaped coffee-pots, jugs, tureens and inkstands. A tall baluster coffee-pot with a plain body and domed cover might only betray that it was made in the rococo period by a bird's eye terminal to the fluted and leaf-surrounded spout. It was often rococo detail rather than rococo design overall that typified the silver of the period, especially silver of a functional nature and silver made for less fashion-conscious or less wealthy clients.

By the 1760's, even the most eager rococoists were tiring of asymmetry. Some silversmiths tended to look again across the Channel and to formalise silver in the French manner once more. Tureens were made shallower, with wavy rims and finials in the form of fruit or vegetables, rather like those made in porcelain. Sometimes ripple-fluted effects were achieved. On occasion, perhaps fostered by Sir Horace Walpole's Strawberry Hill home, there was silver made in the Gothic style. The silver of the late 1750's and the 1760's was silver in a transitional style. It was as though silversmiths were not assured of themselves and were seeking a new theme. Their problems were solved by Robert Adam.

For several years London society had been eloquently discussing and avidly following the excavations of classical sites at Palmyra, Baalbek, Rome and Herculaneum. In 1762 Stuart & Revett added another magnificently illustrated volume to the growing number of books on antiquities for which there was no shortage of subscribers. Artists and architects visited the sites for themselves, and returned with sketches and scale drawings and plenty of ideas to put into practice. Among them was the young Scottish architect, Robert Adam. During four years in Italy between 1754 and 1758 Adam had made careful studies of many classical sites. Under the spell of Herculaneum and Pompeii, Rome and Spalatro, he was very ready to oblige his wealthy London patrons with the new classicism. Adam was fortunate that he very quickly became London's most fashionable designer, and could number the Northumberlands and the Childs of Osterley among his clients. He not only designed houses but took a leading part in interior design as well, planning everything from doors and ceilings to carpets and candelabra. In the eighteenth century, such meddling with other men's crafts mattered less than it did half a century later. When nearly everything was made by hand, the craftsman could easily adapt a design to suit his medium. In the age of the machine, there was a danger that designs were carried out in the wrong materials by the wrong methods. Adam and his circle were also fortunately men of great taste and culture.

The neo-classical approach to antiquity was not bound by any very hard and fast rules. It was rather the application of ideas and of decorative motifs than slavish copying. The acknowledged aim of the neo-classicists was to draw on "the most elegant ornament of the most refined Grecian articles". Laurel wreaths and festoons, anthemion, palmette and scroll borders were neat and restrained after the contorted cult of rococoism. The stone urn and the vase provided an elegant new shape for silver – so few metal-wares had been uncovered in the excavations anyway. Indeed, from wallpaper to cupolas, neo-classicism was application

Adam neo-classicism inspired these candelabra made by Schofield in 1793. Fluting and beading were the favourite ornaments of the period; vase and urn shapes dominated from about 1765 to 1795.

of style rather than imitation, styles in which the first emphasis was on lightness and delicacy.

A development of engraving, called bright-cut, was particularly suited to the Adam designs that soon came to be made in silver. Bright-cut engraving is done with a specially sharp tool which produces a burnished cut, and the effect was excellent for reproducing the garlands and festoons borrowed straight from the books on classical architecture. Fluting was equally suitable for echoing the slender marble pillars and pilasters beloved of Adam, and it was also well suited to the new stamping processes which were being used, especially in Sheffield, for making candlesticks. No one was squeamish about putting machinery to work where the hand craftsman had monopolised before. Indeed, machines were often welcomed as part of progress, and the simplicity of the neo-classical designs and the abundance of them had yet to cause stereotyping, or the tendency to use part of one design allied with part of another without consulting the designer of either.

The very simplicity of the vase and the oval made them suitable for domestic silver such as teapots, tea urns, sugar bowls and swing-handled baskets, soup and sauce tureens as well as for the ubiquitous cups and covers that were presented as race trophies and on every possible civic occasion as well. The classical column was tapered, and topped with an urn finial for candlesticks and candelabra. To be in keeping with the almost stark formality of the oval, beading and reeding were the most favoured border ornaments. Piercing was as restrained as the regular galleried frets of Chinese Chippendale, though the épergne makers, now constrained by the oval and formal classical motifs, did achieve scroll and leaf-pierced borders, and added interest to pierced boat-shapes by using deep-blue glass liners. Piercing had, in fact, undergone a minor revolution with the introduction of the piercing saw, by which woodworking techniques were, in effect, applied to metal.

The success of Adam and the neo-classicists lay in their pretty, delicate designs, but it was too pretty and fragile for many of their contemporaries, both lay and professional. Wyatt and Henry Holland had more grandiose tendencies, while by 1800 even the King voiced an opinion that "the Adams have introduced too much of neatness and prettiness". In silver, however, the "sippets of embroidery" had already started to give way to a grander style by the 1790's. There was more pronounced and even applied decoration overlaying the simplicity of the Grecian. Festoons, once only bright-cut, were now chased with a Roman majesty; small applied medallions, modelled of course on classical lines, were used particularly by Fogelburg and Gilbert on jugs and teapots. Lion masks once again appeared at the knuckles of sauce boats and footed tureens; bold leafage, ovolos and scrolls in relief, and reed and tie borders began to supersede beading and simple reeding. Once again the tide of taste was changing, and sweeping in with the tide, urging it fast ahead, was the Prince of Wales, the last and most powerful of all the great dilettanti.

'Prinny' was an enthusiastic and a lavish patron, though his genius and taste were not always either elegant or wise. He had grandiose schemes for building and furnishing, but changed his mind with infuriating regularity. One day he favoured the Chinese manner, the next the Indian, and then he would veer towards classical Rome or ancient Egypt. But in Rundell & Bridge he found an ambitious firm of goldsmiths who were ready to cater to his strangest whim. They commissioned artists and sculptors to produce designs for plate. Now all sign of Adam grace vanished. "Massiveness," boomed C. H. Tatham, "is the principal characteristic of good Plate," and "good Chasing . . . a branch of Sculpture." At Rundell & Bridge's behest men such as Tatham, John Flaxman and Stothard turned the silversmith into a vehicle for producing sculpture in silver. The old tradition of design evolution, of gradual development vanished. The unhappy, awful situation arose where the specialist in one field dictated to the craftsman in another without understanding either his methods or his material. Fortunately for the reputation of the craft of the silversmith, Rundell & Bridge had at their command a number of excellent workers. In Paul Storr and Benjamin Smith, especially, they had superb craftsmen who were, in fact, capable of translating marble into silver. They achieved magnificence and grandeur particularly through their casting and repoussé chasing which were superlative. The Flaxman chariots, vines and classical figures stood out as though carved in the metal; and by the end of the Peninsular Wars, monumental silver for Wellington was of an unprecedented scale in size, architectural conception and complexity.

In less exalted circles, other silversmiths began to emulate the imposing silverwares sold by Rundell & Bridge. Cast and chased

After the finesse of Adam silver, there was perhaps a natural reaction to grandeur. Largely sponsored by the Royal silversmiths, Rundell, Bridge & Rundell, silver —or, more frequently, silvergilt—became massive and ceremonial. The Prince Regent was a patron who enjoyed this grand style, while it was thought a fitting tribute to the admirals and generals of the period to present them with cups and vases to commemorate their exploits in war. One of the last personal ambassadorial services was that of the Duke, some of it now at Apsley House. This fruit bowl and stand, made by the great Regency silversmith Paul Storr for Rundell, Bridge & Rundell in 1810, stands 13¾ inches high, bears the Royal crest and the crest of Wellesley within the Garter for the Duke.

ornaments, borrowed freely from ancient Rome, Greece, Egypt and Asia Minor, were added to everything from teapots to table centres. Even spoons and forks, simple for so long, were now enriched with palmer's shells and scrolls and dubbed with names like *King's Pattern* and *Queen's Pattern*.

A most distressing habit, in the eyes of the modern collector at any rate, was the 'improving' of old pieces of plain silver by the addition of a revived rococo chasing. This was not only a Victorian weakness, and there are records both of added decoration and alterations made in the period between 1818 and 1830. It was not a practice intended to defraud, but merely to conform to fashion without the additional cost of melting and remaking.

Machines were also being put to work to produce silverwares at a more reasonable price than hand-raising. In Birmingham and Sheffield in particular stamping presses were turning out copies of fashionable silver. For quite a long time, the machine-made products were reasonably well designed. They were often copies of handmade pieces. Sheffield candlesticks were, indeed, good examples of silver made by stamping in sections, assembly and loading. It was later, mostly in the 1830's and after, that there was the temptation to use a base from here, a stem from there, a socket from another design – thus distorting the progress of design and creating a hotch-potch of styles from which the craft is still struggling hard to escape.

The London silversmiths were still, on the whole, hand craftsmen, but they, too, were caught in the net of grandiosity for its own sake. Storr and Smith, who both survived the Regency by many years, were masters of their craft and essayed many pieces – especially after both had broken with Rundell & Bridge – that hinted at the trends the craft might have taken if the silversmiths had been left on their own. Their virtuosity ranged over every style – from noble Roman and elegant Greek to an almost modern simplicity of curves and plain surfaces. They could model the most intricate scenes in relief, they worked silver in chinoiserie designs to resemble carved lacquerware and they reproduced the rococo and the baroque.

Perhaps it was just because they were such superb masters of the craft that they outstripped the ordinary silversmiths whose pace was too slow anyway for the technical changes that were making an onslaught on both the manufacturing and the retail

39

trade. The silversmith was now either a man in his own workshop or one among many in a teeming factory. He no longer was the craftsman selling direct to the customer. His patron was the retailer who would buy, say, his tea services from one maker, his candlesticks from Sheffield, his snuff boxes and vinaigrettes from Birmingham. It was a process that had, in fact, been going on for a long time, though until the nineteenth century, most retail silver dealers had also in fact been silversmiths themselves. They usually took upon themselves the special orders, and bought in only certain wares, such as casters, épergnes, spoons and forks, and other small items. The nineteenth century saw the growth of the shop that was a sales showroom for the wares of a dozen makers.

Sheffield Plate, introduced as a substitute for silver and to provide a wider public with pleasant and decorative wares, was also taking its toll of silver, and in 1840 the introduction of electroplating meant yet another commodity with which silver had to compete. The early Victorian period, with its huge industrial upheavals, its quickly rich and its multiplying poor, changed the face of Britain. The greatest social revolution of all time was in full swing, whirling people into a new way of life – people who had never learnt to appreciate the fine arts. Taste was at a low ebb, worn out by ostentation. Money and the machine began to overwhelm the craftsman, who was always too much of a traditionalist to adapt himself quickly enough to a changing world.

The Victorians did not, however, stifle craftsmanship. They extolled it. They spent long and precious hours working painstakingly on extravagant, monumental and completely non-functional objects for display – exhibition pieces to prove the skill of the craftsman who was losing his place in the commercial scene. Two years before Queen Victoria came to the throne, a 'Select Committee on Arts and Manufactures' was appointed by Parliament. It strongly recommended forging links between fine and applied arts and industrial production: "It equally imports us to encourage art in its loftier attributes," the committee sententiously reported, "since it is admitted that the cultivation of the more exalted branches of design tends to advance the humblest pursuits of industry." But even in 1835, it was almost too late. No exhibition, no laboured patronage could reassemble the shattered fabric of a broken tradition, in which neither design nor craftsmanship followed their original courses.

This rather self-conscious attitude to arts – the consideration that design and form were something apart from function – permeates the whole of the Victorian period. There were, of course, many different styles. Some were factory-produced versions of the silver of the past, with fluted and chased decoration, tolerably reproducing the shells, scalework and flower motifs of the rococo for a new, wide market. Some were almost completely machine-dominated, even to acid-etched decoration and fly-piercing. Handmade silver tended to be the prerogative of London, and sturdy and at times magnificent pieces were made, though towards the end of the century standards unfortunately often dropped, and wares were flimsy, with slender handles, unsteady feet and inapt decoration.

About 1890, retrospection began to play a dominant part in silversmithing. The 1835 Select Committee and, fifteen years later, the campaigning of the Prince Consort had helped to set up the complex of museums that eventually became the several collections at South Kensington. Antiquarian interest in the history of the goldsmith's craft aroused new interest, especially in the mediaeval and renaissance periods. The age of collecting had arrived. Since the first collectors were also the men who before had been the chief patrons of the silversmith, there was a natural tendency for the craftsmen to cater for their antiquarian tastes. Pre-Raphaelite influence extended, of course, to metalwork, but in silver there were also new schools of design whose influence has survived to this day. Guilds of artist-craftsmen sprang up in London, Birmingham and Glasgow. They trained young men in design and in silversmithing, seeking to release the craft from the tentacles of industrial soullessness. All their efforts, however, did not link design and industry, though it did start the process that is now beginning to have its effect.

The general output of silver remained chiefly a watered-down version of previous work. The manufacturing silversmiths' pattern books were an amalgam of antique silver and attempts to produce pieces that were 'modern'. But there was a gulf still between the designers and the makers. On the one hand there was too much emphasis on the hand craftsman, on the other a rejection of what the down-to-earth manufacturer considered, at times justifiably, to be 'arty-crafty'. Today some of that feeling still lingers on, though a growing number of manu-facturers are aware of the need for designers and in fact employ them, either on their staff or in a consultative capacity. There are still plenty of designers who scorn industry, and who labour on producing specialist silverwares. There is, of course, room for both, and some of our best contemporary silversmiths divide their time between industry, training new men and designing special pieces. For the silversmith today has no longer the great private patron. His patrons are the manufacturers and, largely by the encouragement of craftsmanship schemes by the Worship-ful Company of Goldsmiths, industrial concerns and civic authorities. A growing awareness of design among the general public augurs well for those silversmiths who realise that proper use of machines and technical advances, allied with good, functional design, will bring the public back as the great patron of one of the oldest applied arts in the world.

2

TECHNIQUES OF THE SILVERSMITH

An understanding of the way silverwares are made and decorated is essential to the wise collector who desires a knowledge of the development of silver styles. Though the actual processes of making a piece of silver have changed little over the centuries, there are variations, particularly in the methods of decoration, that should be noted. The ability to recognise how a piece was made is often a useful means of dating unmarked or partly marked silver. Armed with such knowledge, the collector has a strong shield against the faker and the forger, whose work, mostly of late nineteenth and early twentieth century date, usually betrays an ignorance of the finer points of silver design and manufacture.

For centuries, the prime tool of the silversmith has been the hammer. It still is today. Some tasks have become somewhat less onerous through the introduction of machines, but on the whole mechanisation has been very limited, and machines are rarely used in the production of high-grade silverwares. It is rather in the manufacture and preparation of the raw material that the advances of science in the past three hundred years have most noticeably helped the modern silversmith. Indeed, processes and tools alike are often those used a hundred or more years ago, and many methods can be traced back to an almost forgotten past in the prehistory of Egypt and other civilisations of the Middle East.

Today, for instance, the silversmith has no longer to cast his own ingots – unless he does so by choice. Before the introduction of modern refining methods in the late nineteenth century, silver was extracted from the ore with nitric acid. This dissolved out all base metals present, but any gold remained, usually in very small quantities. Until the last century, the mines of Mexico, Peru and Bolivia provided almost all the silver worked in Europe, and even today, though Australia and America are the largest producers, Mexican silver remains the purest available.

From very early times it was recognised that silver needed to be alloyed with another metal to make it hard enough for use, whether as coinage or for decorative or domestic purposes. Probably dating back to the Saxon moneyers, and certainly firmly established by the end of the twelfth century, alloying with copper to sterling standard was usual in Britain. Sterling silver contains 925 parts pure silver to 75 parts copper. Expressed in Troy weight, the ancient system still used for gold and silver, this gives eleven ounces, two pennyweights (dwts.) pure silver to eighteen pennyweights of copper, making up a Troy pound of twelve ounces. The resulting metal is malleable yet durable, takes a good polish and is of a fine grey lustre.

In Britain the Britannia standard is the only other one permitted for silver. It has a higher silver content (eleven ounces, ten pennyweights to the Troy pound – or, 958 parts per 1000), and was first introduced in 1697 to prevent, as previously stated, the silversmiths from using the sterling coinage of the country to make silverwares. Sometimes known as *New Standard* or *Better Nine*, it was obligatory from 1697 until 1720, and has been in optional use since then. It is marked with a figure of Britannia seated and a lion's head erased instead of the sterling standard lion passant and the leopard's head mark.

The silversmith of the past had to alloy his own metal, cast it into brick-like ingots and then prepare it for working by the laborious hammering process known as battery. Until the invention of the rolling mill – the first one was noted in Surrey towards the end of the seventeenth century – hammering out the ingots into flattish workable sheets was the only available method. For nearly all silver hollow-wares, which is the term used for jugs, pots, cups, bowls, dishes and trays, the starting point is a flat sheet of silver. Hand-forged spoons and forks, however, are still made from the ingot or from a piece of rough drawn wire. Small objects such as knops, finials and small articles such as candlesticks are frequently made by casting. Spinning and stamping also have their place in the silversmith's workshop, the former now being quite extensively used in the production of silver hollow-wares, the latter a relatively modern process introduced about 1770.

The making of silverware by hand has not changed except in minor details for hundreds of years. Taking a sheet of suitable gauge silver, generally a circle, the silversmith first shapes it by hammering it into a depression in a wooden block, gradually working it row by row from the outer edge inwards with a sinking hammer. Each successive row is, of course, the width of only one hammer blow (all the hammers used by the silversmith, light or heavy, for shaping or decorating, are double-headed to give better balance). This blocking process produces a shallow saucer shape, and the shaping is continued over a leather pad filled with sand (known as a saddle), using the ball-ended sinking-hammer. If the ware is a bowl shape, it can be entirely made by this process, which is then known as sinking.

The hammering, which is always worked row by row, has the effect of hardening as well as shaping the silver, and to offset this brittling, the metal has to be annealed from time to time; by heating it to a dull red heat and then cooling it, the silver becomes tough and malleable once more. In the modern silversmith's workshop, gas furnaces are usual for annealing, but formerly the fire had to be coaxed with bellows and blowpipes, and a scale of copper oxide, known as 'fire', was the usual result.

This does occur even with modern furnaces, but in the past it was inevitable, and much time must have been spent in cleaning off the oxide by 'boiling out' in weak acid and scouring the surface.

Most wares are too deep and narrow to be made entirely by sinking, and they are raised over a stake or anvil. The saucer shape is reversed and held over a suitable metal stake which may be one of a dozen or more of different sizes and shapes. The silversmith works not from the edge but from the base, again working row by row, but coaxing the metal towards the rim. As the top edge is reached, it is hammered down to thicken it, a process variously called corking or caulking. This gives a strong, firm edge to the top of the ware.

There is one exception to the corking process – in the making of tumbler cups, in which a thickened base is needed to give the cup balance. The silversmith therefore hammers the silver back again to the base, instead of working up to the top each time.

In hand-raising, great care must be taken to ensure that the silver is of even and correct thickness, especially when the body is curved or swaged. Even for apparently simple wares the smith has to go over the work eight or nine times to bring the shallow saucer shape up to a tall form, and between each course the silver must be kept malleable by annealing and cleaning. Cleanliness of tools is also essential, or the surface of the silver will be irreparably marred. Each time the silversmith takes up his hammer to start work again, he cleans both tool-head and stake with a very fine, old piece of emery paper to keep them perfectly free from dirt or rust, and hammerheads are always kept covered when not in use.

The supreme test of good silversmithing is flat hammering – the making of trays, salvers and waiters. Unlike most hollow-wares, the border, often a cast one or of wire, must be soldered on first of all. The process immediately causes the whole piece to buckle, and the larger the tray or salver, the more it will

Most silverwares start from a circular sheet of silver, which must be hammered into a saucer shape over a wooden block. Bowls can be made entirely by sinking them over a leather pad, or saddle, working the metal gradually row by row from the centre outwards.

Most wares are too deep and narrow to be worked entirely by sinking. So the silver is reversed and held over a stake or anvil, and, still working row by row but now from the base towards the top, the silversmith *raises* the ware, coaxing the metal to shape with every blow.

buckle under the heat. Before that is corrected, however, the silversmith hammers out the bouge, or edge, of the piece. A dish or waiter with a regular oval or circular well that does not follow the form of the border is easiest to hammer out, but most salvers are made with shaped borders such as the pie-crust or Chippendale styles so frequently, and superbly, made in the eighteenth century. After shaping, the whole piece has to be hammered absolutely flat, yet every stroke of the hammer must work the silver away to the edge and the shape of the border. One false stroke and the whole piece may be spoiled irretrievably.

Many pieces such as tall coffee-pots and tankards have long been made by a more labour-saving process than raising. A flat sheet of silver is first turned up into a cone and soldered. The seam can sometimes be detected inside a pot or tankard along the line of the handle. Further hammering shapes the piece as required, and the bottom must be let in and soldered. Since there is no thickened top edge, a solid wire mount has to be fitted. Nearly all flat-based wares are made by this method, and the soldered-in base is easily detected by the slight bumps of solder, in early pieces often left quite rough.

A mechanical method of making silver hollow-wares is by spinning, which was known even in early Egyptian times. The silver is held firmly against a shaped wooden chuck and the spinning tool, supported firmly under the spinner's arm, is pressed hard against the metal as the lathe rotates. As with hand-raising, the tool works the metal from the base to the top edge, so that a good thick edge can be obtained provided the body metal is of heavy gauge. Formerly, spun silverwares had to be hammered after forming in order to harden the metal, but today specially hard silver is available for spinning.

When the silver has been shaped, it presents a somewhat rough surface, due to the hammering processes. It must therefore be smoothed by a process known as planishing, which is yet another hammering process. Planishing is, in effect, polishing with a hammer – the silver is smoothed and unevennesses polished out of the surface with light, deft strokes. Inside hand-raised wares, the heavier marks of the raising hammer can often still be seen.

The casting of metals (all ingots are of course cast) has been known since very early times. Silversmiths use the method known as sand-casting for all kinds of small parts and objects. A pattern is first carefully made in metal, wood, plaster or modelling wax, and embedded in a special sand, called marl. Sometimes steatite or cuttlefish-bone are used. The sand or other material is held in an iron case made in two halves; the model is placed up to its centre in the lower half of the case – the sand and model alike being dusted with charcoal or burnt brick to form a parting surface. The top half is then clamped over the lower half to take an impression. The case is then parted, the model removed and the sand dried hard. It is then clamped together again, and molten metal poured into the case will run into the cavities left by the model, taking up every detail. There will be some minor roughness and faults – perhaps a few pit marks and a line visible along the parting surface – which must be cleaned up afterwards. Several small articles or parts can be made at one time by this method, each separate one being united by small channels, known as gates, or gets, which are cut away later.

Stamping of parts was first introduced in the silver trade in Birmingham in the third quarter of the eighteenth century. Buttons and other small objects were stamped out, and the standard of die-making at that period was exceptionally high. Soon the process was extended to other wares, and in Sheffield the stampers were particularly noted for their candlesticks. These were made in sections, assembled, and loaded with a resinous pitch substance to give them strength and stability.

Hollow-wares can also be made by stamping and other mechanical methods, and since the nineteenth century the process has indeed been applied to teapots, basins and so on, producing cheap silverwares for a large market. Stamping processes are not, however, really suited to silver wares of any size, and if hand-raising is not feasible, then spinning and hand-finishing are usually preferable.

Stamping of wires, over a die, has largely in modern times been superseded by rolled wires. The stamped patterns on early silver can often be detected by minor breaks, the mounts often being produced in only short lengths. Cast wires and other mounts were also much used in the eighteenth century and wire-drawing is one of the oldest methods of making wires. It was in use in England during the Tudor period, and wires fine enough for filigree work can be drawn. A piece of silver rod is tapered at one end, and then drawn through holes of diminishing size in the draw-plate. As with hammering, drawing tends to harden the metal, which has to be annealed from time to time during the process.

The soldering of handles, feet, spouts, foot rings and other parts in silver is a much more skilled operation than it first appears to the layman. A neat joint is the pride of every silver-smith, and it redounds to the credit of the craftsmen of the past that they managed to achieve neat joints, sometimes almost invisible, with the rather clumsy and inaccurate bellows blow-pipe. Today the modern gas blowpipe and even cleaner oxygen blowpipe still need considerable skill on the part of the solderer.

Old solder is often quite easy to detect, because of its charac-teristic colour, caused by working over a charcoal flame, and the use of brass as the alloying metal rather than the whiter zinc used nowadays. The inadequacy of the old blowpipes also meant that the silversmith tended to use more solder than was ab-solutely necessary, and often the marks where excess solder was turned away can be seen on the bases of coffee-pots and bowls.

Once all the parts – body, foot-ring, handle-sockets, spout and so on – have been soldered together, they are sent to the Assay Office for testing and hallmarking. Each maker applies his own registered mark, and once the authorities at the Assay Office have assured themselves that the metal used throughout is of the correct standard, they apply the hallmarks indicating the stan-dard, the place at which it was assayed, and the date. When a piece has been assayed, no further additions may be made without returning it for further assaying. It is simply cleaned up, polished and finished – perhaps with one of the many decorative processes that help to make period silver so very distinctive.

Several types of decoration are, of course, applied before the silver is sent for assay – applied wires, cut-card work and cast applied ornament. Most embossed chasing and repoussé work is also done before assaying, and this can often be detected as pre-assay by the fact that the hallmarks are struck over the decoration.

Applied decoration (which must be soldered to the ware), chased ornament (which is achieved by means of hammer and punch), and piercing and engraving (which entail the removal of metal), are the three basic methods by which silver can be decorated. Sometimes, silver is left plain, devoid of any ornament. Sometimes its surface is almost wholly concealed by the use of one or even a combination of all three types of decoration. Some forms are typical of an identifiable period, and can be used to guide the collector faced with an unmarked piece. To the practised eye, there is something very different between the rococo chasing of the 1740's and that of its imitators seventy or eighty years later. Many details have always remained uncopied, either from inability to do so or from clashes of taste. There has been no revival, for instance, of seventeenth-century cast caryatid handles, or of the delicate and intricately pierced applied work with tiny medallion heads and masks favoured in the 1720's.

The earliest form of decoration was engraving. Its scope extends from a few scratched lines or a clumsily inscribed set of initials to the consummate artistry of the early eighteenth century masters, led by Simon Gribelin and William Hogarth; these men used their gravers as if they were pencils, and made linear decoration superbly fluid and full of movement. To impart suggestions of light and shade by turning the sharp tool within the cut without producing a ragged edge requires great skill, and the engraver has to employ many types of scriber and graver, according to the width and depth of cut required.

The essentially linear technique of engraving tends to make for simplified ornament – except in the exquisite pictorial engravings and the fine armorials of the eighteenth-century masters. Naturally, commemorative and other inscriptions were early put to decorative use on silver, one of the most effective uses of lettering appearing on the late fourteenth-century Studley Bowl (now in the Victoria & Albert Museum). Amid most ordered foliage, the letters of the alphabet appear on bowl and cover –

**Detail of engraving (see plate 58),
credibly attributed to Hogarth.**

perhaps a tribute in silver-gilt to an unknown scribe or scholar.

During the second half of the sixteenth century, engraved ornament was often in the form of a band of foliate scrolls within a simple border of strapwork, sometimes with a pendant of leafage extending from the interlacing of the strapwork. This was the almost standard form of decoration on the Elizabethan communion cups made to replace the chalices condemned by the reforming bishops. In secular silver, engraved strapwork and scrolling foliage remained popular and appeared on wine cups, shallow-footed bowls, beakers, tankards, dishes and bell salts from the 1580's to the middle of the seventeenth century.

About 1680 there was a fashion for engraving of a type that seems to be peculiar to England – engravings of figures, animals, birds, trees, flowers, foliage and even temples and pavilions in the Chinese taste. Most combine a naïve style of workmanship with an exotic charm, and these often rather sketchily-drawn chinoiseries had a vogue for about fifteen years, appearing on all kinds of silverware, from small cups, mugs, beakers and small boxes to porringers, tankards, salvers and, most notable of all, on the large toilet sets of the 1680's. Similar chinoiseries were often flat chased.

Alongside this rather exceptional engraving, there was the more pedestrian but often well-executed use of the skill for crests and armorials. These were considered a very necessary addition to silver in ages that were more conscious than modern times of family connections, and they were also a useful way of denoting ownership. Study of the styles of coats-of-arms and the types of lettering used for inscriptions at different periods can prove both interesting and useful to the silver collector. Not all the armorials on silver are contemporary with the piece – indeed, most are later and may even replace earlier coats erased to make way for those of new owners. Sometimes, however, the armorials constitute an integral part of the design or decoration of a piece of silver, and during the first half of the eighteenth century they were occasionally cast, chased and applied. Engraving remained, however, more usual, either as an addition or as original work. An engraved coat-of-arms on a tankard of 1685 provides the centrepiece for the whole ornament of the piece, for its berried mantling extends broadly over the body of the tankard (page 60.)

The early eighteenth century saw engraving at its most

In engraving decoration is produced by cutting away the surface.

spectacular and finest. This was, in fact, the great era of all the
decorative arts – piercing, applied decoration, and chasing as
well. The skill of the silver engravers has never been equalled,
let alone surpassed. Though few pieces can with certainty be
ascribed to individual masters, this was the age of Simon Gribelin,
a Huguenot engraver of inimitable skill. A few of his pieces have
been identified, and there are prints and proofs of his work in
the British Museum. His contemporaries included Benjamin
Rhodes, author of a little book of cyphers and monograms
published in 1723, and himself a practical engraver; Joseph
Sympson, another engraver who produced a book of cyphers;
and William Hogarth, apprenticed to silversmith Ellis Gamble,
though it is doubtful that he kept up his connection with the
silver trade for very long. These men and others whose names
are unrecorded were working at a time when painstakingly
precise and complicated ornament was coming into fashion.
With skill and patience they achieved shell, scroll and strapwork
borders and, in addition to elaborate insignia and armorials, at
times produced most complex and exquisite pictorial engraving.
 Engraving, other than for armorials and crests, tended to

wane in the period of the high rococo, but with Adam the fine line of the graver could more readily echo the shallow neo-classical outlines than the chasing tool. About 1780, the variation known as bright-cut engraving added a new brilliance to engraved ornament. It has an unmistakably clear-cut and brilliant appearance due to contrasting depths of cut, the very highly polished tool picking out the silver with one edge and burnishing the channel left with the other. It was a technique especially suited to festoons and for the outline borders surrounding the fashionable pierced work of the period from about 1780 to 1810.

A mechanical development of engraving is the decoration known as engine-turning. Complicated lathes for turning and for surface decoration were a feature of the silversmith's workshop as early as the seventeenth century, but it was in the second half of the eighteenth that the application of the lathe to decoration really came into its own. Smallworkers in London and, still more extensively, in Birmingham, applied engine-turned patterns to all sorts of boxwares such as vinaigrettes, snuff boxes, perfume bottle holders, even to the extent of arranging two, four or even half a dozen different patterns of turning on a single small box. The work is mounted on pitch and held in a chuck which brings the silver to the cutting tool. By arranging for the tool also to move, different patterns can be cut.

Though often used in conjunction with engraving, piercing is quite a different technique of decoration by removing metal; it is also one of the techniques in which the method of working changed during the second half of the eighteenth century. Originally, pierced decoration was done with chisels, punching the silver away into a variety of patterns, at times very fine and intricate. Silver table-baskets are recorded from the late sixteenth century onwards (there is one of 1597 in the Victoria & Albert Museum), and during the middle years of the seventeenth century pierced work in conjunction with embossed chased work was used in their decoration. The Charles II period saw the earliest casters, their tops and often their bases also pierced out in rather coarse stars, hearts, crescents and scroll shapes. By the end of the century, the silversmiths had mastered new skills in piercing, and casters in particular were often provided with very finely pierced tops in flower and leaf designs, and even with minute figures, producing delightful and lacy effects.

Pierced work for casters, baskets and strainers remained of a high order during the early part of the eighteenth century. Piercing was usually done after assay, with the resultant loss in the pierced designs of the hallmarks, sometimes partly, occasionally wholly cut away in the scrolls and dots of the punch-work.

During the 1770's new techniques for achieving openwork silverwares changed the whole style of the craft. One was the tendency to build up the sides of baskets from wire, pierced section or galleries. Another was the introduction of the saw-piercing frame. Saw-piercing is the method still used today on finely fretted, hand-pierced wares. A tiny hole is drilled in the silver, on to which the design to be cut has been impressed in a thin layer of wax. The slender saw blade is slipped into the hole and clamped into the frame. The piercer cuts away his design, holding his saw absolutely vertically, and tending to bring the work to the saw rather than the saw to the work. Broken saws are frequent. Very delicate and intricate patterns can be cut by this method, and on comparing chisel-pierced and saw-pierced silver, a keen eye can easily detect whether the silver has been punched back with a chisel or if the tiny teeth of a hacksaw have bitten their way into the edges of the silver.

Modern saw-piercing is still well done, although the exponents of the craft, like those of engraving, are few. Too often modern piercing is the soulless and mechanical punch-piercing of the fly-press, which produces even coarser cuts than the early punch-piercing, at which craftsmen soon achieved a skill even finer than that of modern saw-piercing.

Formerly piercing was done with
small chisels. Since the second half
of the eighteenth century, however, saw piercing has been usual.
The piercing saw may also be
needed for cutting designs or for
cut-card work—as shown above.

A form of ornament introduced from France about 1650 and
also reliant on the skill of the piercer is cut-card work. Nowadays, the thin cards are cut to shape with the piercing saw, but
formerly, as with piercing, they were chisel-cut to shape. The
cards are very thin plates of silver cut into silhouettes – often
based on leaf shapes – and then soldered on to the bases or round

the knobs on the covers of bowls, tankards, flagons, ewers and boxes, and often at the junctions of handles and spouts of tea-pots and coffee-pots. This applied decoration, which of course was an integral part of the ware, had to be done before it went for assay and marking. Towards the end of the century and later, during the supremacy of the immigrant Huguenot crafts-man, cut-card and other applied ornament was of a very high order. Fine and intricate patterns of scrollwork and foliage needed exceptional skill in application to ensure that no solder crept out from behind the design, which had to be kept flat and appear integrated with the surface. This was especially difficult when another part, such as a foot ring, had to be soldered on afterwards.

Applied ornament during the 1720's and later was often of an extremely delicate and detailed nature. Sometimes it was cast and then chased with details, sometimes it was stamped, often it was pierced. Casting, for many years used for small objects and parts such as knobs, handles and the like, was much used for the applied strapwork, the palmate leaves and the human and lion masks favoured by the Huguenot designers. As the eighteenth century wore on, so castings became more elaborate, and rich mounts became an essential part of the silversmith's repertoire, as well as rich designs, often asymmetrical, for heavy cast candlesticks.

There are three types of chasing. One is a surface decoration, known as flat chasing, which is often unwittingly confused with engraving. In chasing, however, the process pushes the metal into pattern, but does not remove any of it, whereas engraving does. The second type of chasing is often known as embossed or repoussé chasing. Thirdly, there is the process loosely known as cast chasing.

Like engraving, embossing is a very ancient form of decoration. At its simplest it is a series of bosses pushed up into patterns from the back of the piece. For detail and interest, those bosses must be given further definition by working on them with hammer and punches from the front – the process known as repoussé. The chaser uses hundreds of different punches to achieve different effects. Some of his tools are far older than he, perhaps as much as two centuries old; others he makes himself for a particular job. But whatever his tool, it must be properly used. Even the boldest design is the outcome of small, even and regular punches; heavy, clumsy strokes would completely ruin the design.

To achieve the domed bosses that form the basic outlines of embossed work, the silver is laid face downwards on a bed of pitch or soft wood. For enclosed shapes such as jugs or tankards, however, initial embossing has to be done 'by remote control' using a snarling iron. This is a length of iron firmly held in the bench vice, its head domed according to the pattern and depth of boss required. The silver is held over the domed head, and the iron arm of the tool tapped with a hammer so that the head chatters and bumps out a curve in the silver.

For repoussé chasing, chasing up castings and for flat chasing, the silver is either filled with pitch or supported on a bed of pitch, and this in turn is placed on a half-shot held in a leather ring. Thus the craftsman is enabled to turn the work as he requires it. In almost all decorative processes used by the silver-smith, the work is brought to the tool rather than the tool to the work. Very intricate designs can be achieved with both repoussé and flat chasing. In repoussé work, undercuts are sometimes made to give great relief definition. Flat-chased designs are often traced on and then the pattern gently pushed into shape using fine tools and tiny movements. Never is any metal removed, it is merely gently coaxed into patterns. Matted effects, giving a textured ground, are also a form of chasing. Giving definition to castings is also done with chasing tools. It may be simply cleaning up the outlines of a cast baluster candlestick, the defining of fluting or it may be the detailed outlining of a lion or human head mask, a riot of marine motifs or the minute delineation of

Embossed Chasing

a complete figure. The silversmith rarely uses carving to achieve his effects in relief. More usually, he does it by chasing.

Embossed chased swags of fruit, leaves and flowers, often set against matted backgrounds, were typical of the late Renaissance silver of the Tudor period in England. During the reign of Charles I there was introduced a Dutch style of chasing, the work of Van Vianen and his followers, with naturalistic motifs in swirling styles, flowers, foliage, scrolls and masks much in demand. After the Restoration, chased motifs in the Dutch style were revived, the boldly embossed designs serving to conceal the

Top left : **The chaser can achieve a wide variety of designs using many different punches with which he coaxes the metal into the required pattern. In chasing, no metal is removed.** *Top right :* **detail of the applied chased ornament and matted groundwork on the Sutherland wine cistern by Paul De Lamerie (see page 26).** *Bottom left :* **a modern cast chased detail—a dolphin finial on a bowl and cover designed and made by Omar Ramsden in 1929.**

Left : **Tankard of 1685 showing the crisp appearance of engraving. Both the coat-of-arms and its extensive berried mantling are engraved.** *Right :* **in contrast, the softer appearance achieved by flat chasing on a chinoiserie tankard made only two years earlier.**

thin gauge of silver and to cater for the patrons' love of display.

Chasing remained an important decorative feature throughout the baroque period, and fine fluted work and acanthus leaf decoration exerted the skills of the chasers. When the Huguenots began to settle in England about 1680, the newest French designs were often based on scroll and strapwork motifs carried out in high relief. Some exceptional chasing in this *Régence* manner was accomplished by the Huguenot masters, notably by Pierre Harache. But about 1700, taste began to veer towards a restrained style, relying on moulded forms and a minimum of chased work. The chaser was, for the time being, restricted to work on castings and the occasional definition of simple applied motifs such as lion masks, shell and human-head masks, flying-figure handles and so on.

Early Georgian flat chasing followed the formal *Régence* designs that had been occasionally interpreted in high relief at the turn of the century. Strapwork enclosing shells, scrolls and foliage was immaculately executed in flat chasing. Heads, pendant husks, and armorials were likewise exquisitely flat-chased, their softer outlines, formal and precise though they were, making an excellent foil for the crisper detail of engraving with which flat chasing was not infrequently associated. The square Walpole Salver, made by Paul De Lamerie in 1728, exemplifies the skills of the chaser in the detailed cast shells and *guilloche* border around the upcurved rim, which is flat chased with a band of trelliswork divided by male and female portrait busts. An inner border combines flat chasing and engraving in a most elaborate style, while the centre of the salver, understandably accredited to William Hogarth, is engraved with a great circular medallion of considerable detail. A representation of both faces of the Exchequer Seal of George I is surrounded by views of London and classical figures. The salver, made for Robert Walpole, is now in the Victoria & Albert Museum.

Such combining of the skills of the chaser and engraver was

gradually ousted by the advent of the richly decorative rococo style. Here the chaser almost wholly dominated, creating in high relief, at first fairly ordered, more latterly highly exuberant designs based on swirling, naturalistic, marine and other motifs. Casting was extensively employed throughout the period, producing elaborate candlesticks and candelabra, sometimes with figure stems, applied motifs in high relief, finials in the form of fruit, vegetables or even animals and birds, and most detailed applied mounts.

About 1750, the turbulent movement inherent in rococo design began to cloy, and some silversmiths looked once more to a less exaggerated style, though still much ornamented. The chaser was still in the lead, but about 1760 he had to give way to the engraver. The grace and lightness of Robert Adam's pencil was reproduced by the engraver of silver, and when depth or contrasts were needed, even they were achieved by engraving, not chasing.

Chasing is, however, always so much a part of silversmithing that it was not long in abeyance. Fluting gave the chaser an opening, and soon festoons and classical borders, skilfully chased, were making their appearance on the vase-inspired cups and bowls of the Adam period. Gradually Rome took over from Greece, and decoration became bolder and heavier – to the advantage of the chaser. By 1800, the chaser was striding into his own again – with a vengeance. During the Regency the art of chasing was of a very high order. The designs of the sculptors Flaxman, Tatham and Stothard demanded exceptional skill on the part of the chaser, who had to interpret sculpture in silver – modelling, casting and chasing designs that were often more appropriate to marble or other stone. The grandeur of the innumerable Warwick Vases in silver, copied from the marble at Warwick Castle, bears witness to the skill and patience of the chasers. That skill has survived today in the accurate and detailed models of birds and animals still made by a few of the London silversmiths, and in the work of a few outstanding modern silver designers, chiefly for commissions of ceremonial plate.

The rise and recession of different kinds of decoration on silver is often allied to the taste for simplicity or grandeur. The great ages of embossed chased, repoussé chased and cast chased work are, by and large, those of display – Tudor, early Stuart, Charles II, rococo and Regency. These, too, are the ages when gilding was also much in favour, adding richness to the display created by the ornament, though certainly in early times, gilding was often simply a practical form of protection from tarnishing.

Gilding nowadays is chiefly done electrolytically. This is a safe and satisfactory method, though very often the effect is marred by using a very dark yellow or reddish gold. The older, and very unhealthy, mercurial gilding generally imparted a much paler, lemon hue to the silver, very readily distinguishable from its modern counterpart. Old gilding is naturally often worn, and so assumes a softer and more pleasant appearance. Part-, or parcel-gilding, with certain parts of the ware picked out in gilding, is an effective technique rarely met with nowadays, but which was popular in the Elizabethan period. Then, as now, it was often simply a matter of personal taste whether a piece of silver should be treated with gilding, much as there is a choice between mirror polishing and satin-finish for 'white' plate.

Good polishing is an essential factor in the appearance of silver. The ordeal by hammer and fire leaves the silver dull and lustreless. In general, buffing with an abrasive powder against a rotating leather-covered wooden wheel is the only preliminary treatment needed for silver. Pumice and fine sand are used for this first buffing, then finely ground limestone powder and a felt wheel, or dolly, complete the polishing process. Final finishing – which must incidentally be done before engraved decoration is added – is done with rouge. The best hand polishers use the fleshy part of the hand or the forearm. Care has to be taken during the polishing and finishing processes that as little of the metal as possible is removed – quite considerable proportions, up to as much as nine per cent, may be lost in the process. Intricate, chased patterns require special polishing, and crevices and corners have often to be burnished by rubbing with an agate or a steel burnisher.

Turned-wood handles and knobs for teapots and coffee-pots have been favoured since the end of the eighteenth century, though silver handles and ivory handles have also always had their adherents. Ivory during the early part of the century was usually used in its natural colour, but later, ivory stained green was a pleasant innovation that had the advantage of avoiding discoloration. Throughout the century, many handles of tea- and coffee-pots, kettles and argyles were bound with wicker – a steady source of custom for at least one basketmaker whose account books show several silversmiths among his Soho customers.

In more recent years, bone, fibre and man-made materials such as xylonite and nylon have been generally used for handles, though for silver hollow-ware ivory and wood (and, of course, silver) remain the most important, while for flatware and cutlery, silver, mother-of-pearl and ivory still have their place, according to the use to which the ware will be put.

3

HALLMARKS—THEIR USES AND ABUSES

For centuries, the buyer of silver has been safeguarded by the hallmarking laws and by the regulation of the craft of the goldsmith and silversmith by the trade guilds. The marking of plate is probably of very ancient origin. It is apparent that there was some form of control as early as Roman and Byzantine times, and certainly in most countries of Europe systems of testing and marking wares made of precious metals were ordained from the early mediaeval period.

The hallmarks on silver are primarily intended as a guarantee of the standard of the metal used. Only incidentally have they provided the other information about date and maker that has proved so invaluable to the silver collector. Indeed, it is only a little over a hundred years since the antiquarian, Octavius Morgan, published his findings that the alphabetical letters included in the series of marks punched on at the London Assay Office had been applied in regular cycles not only during the nineteenth century but for hundreds of years. Every aspect of the hallmark and the maker's mark – the type of letter, the form of the shields, the appearance of the lion and the variations in the town mark as well as the details of the maker's mark – need careful study and assessment by the silver collector. They are an important guide to genuineness. But they are only a guide. For too much attention to the marks may, in fact, prove more of a bane than a blessing. Hallmarks are only part of the story of

66

silver. A piece can rarely stand on the importance of the marks alone, unless they are very rare ones (and there are many exceptionally fine pieces of genuine silver that have, for one reason or another, escaped the process of marking). Moreover, they can be and have been forged, transposed and altered to suit the nefarious purposes of the faker.

On the whole, however, hallmarking has proved in England to be a very effective safeguard. Since mediaeval times, the laws have been fairly strict, and punishment heavy. A proper study of hallmarking allied to an appreciation of styles and methods of making provides a strong shield against the faker, for few forgers are knowledgeable enough to contrive pieces that not only appear to carry the correct marks in the correct position, but are right in every detail of design and decoration.

The history of the hallmarking system in England is more than six and a half centuries old, while the first ordinance setting up the standard for silverwares dates from 1238, in the reign of Henry III. This referred specifically to London, and commanded the Mayor and Aldermen to select six discreet goldsmiths to superintend the craft. It was almost a century later that the Goldsmiths' Craft of London received its first Royal Charter.

The first major statute decreeing that a mark should be used on silver was that of Edward I in 1300. Under this law, all silver had to be assayed by the Guardians of the Craft and marked with the leopard's head before it was to be allowed to "depart out of the hands of the workers". This ordinance applied not only to London but "in all good towns of England where there are goldsmiths they shall make the same statutes . . . and that one shall go from each town for all the others to London to seek their sure touch". The leopard was, of course, the royal lion, but the 1300 statute does not make it clear whether it was reserved for London only, or, indeed, whether the London goldsmiths had jurisdiction over provincial craftsmen. Certainly London took to itself the leopard's head mark, using it as the town mark, although originally it appears to have been ordained as the standard mark.

The next mark to be specified by law was the maker's mark. In 1363 Edward III laid down "that each Master Goldsmith shall have a mark to himself" which was to be registered with the Guardians of the Craft superintending the Assay or testing of the wares. In early days silversmiths' marks, rather like merchants' marks, were more usually signs and symbols than sets of initials.

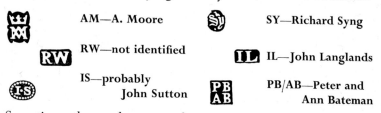

AM—A. Moore   SY—Richard Syng

RW—not identified   IL—John Langlands

IS—probably John Sutton   PB/AB—Peter and Ann Bateman

Sometimes the mark was a rebus or a pun on the craftsman's name, giving a faint clue to identity at times, often it was a mark derived from the goldsmith's shop sign. Unhappily, though many lists of goldsmiths all over the country have survived, few can with certainty be ascribed any particular marks, even as late as the seventeenth century, when initials were more often coming into use. In 1697, when the Act decreeing a higher standard of silver for manufactured wares came into force, makers had to re-register their marks using the first two letters of their surname. This often confusing method did not deter them from incorporating symbols, and it is noteworthy that many silversmiths of French extraction continued the French practice of using a fleur-de-lys, crown and two dots in relatively large punches. As late as 1728 James Maitland placed a grasshopper above his initials, for he worked at the sign of the Grasshopper in Suffolk Street. Indeed, even after craftsmen were ordered to re-register their marks in the form of initials of forename and surname in 1739, many chose to continue to add a small crown, star or other symbol to their punch.

Despite the regulations, there were various complaints about the sale of sub-standard wares, and the gilding and silvering of base metal, both of which were formerly illegal. By the fifteenth century, the hallmarking scheme was virtually established. A statute of 1423 confirmed the use of the sterling standard for all silverwares, and ordained that no "workmanship of silver" was to be "set to sale" in the city of London unless it bore the leopard's head and the maker's mark. By the same statute, York, Newcastle-upon-Tyne, Norwich, Lincoln, Bristol, Coventry and Salisbury were set up as assay towns, "each having divers touches", though in 1462 the Goldsmiths' Company of London was empowered with the right of search, inspection and regulation of all "sorts of gold and silver" set to sale throughout the country.

In 1477 another Statute made it incumbent upon the Goldsmiths' Company of London to ensure that the standard be maintained. Within a year the date-letter system was fully established, though it is more than probable that some such system of dating by using letters of the alphabet had been put to use by the goldsmiths some years earlier. From 1478 until the present day, clear and regular cycles of letters have been used, giving an unparalleled method of dating. In London, a twenty-year cycle, omitting J and the five letters from V to Z is used, though in other towns the systems varied, just as the number of towns charged with assaying plate varied over the years.

In 1544 a fourth mark made its appearance along with the maker's mark and the hallmarks. This was the lion passant gardant crowned (that is, a crowned lion looking over its shoulder). No one knows quite how the mark came to be used, the most likely theory being that the Goldsmiths' Company took it as a standard mark to indicate that the silver was of the proper sterling standard in an age when the coinage, which Henry VIII had debased, was not. The lion remained crowned only for a few years; from 1550 it was a simple lion passant gardant until

1821, when it became a lion passant (with the head in profile).

Lion passant gardent crowned (to 1550)

Lion passant gardant (to 1821)

Lion passant (1821 — present)

With the establishment by Act of Parliament in 1696 of the higher Britannia standard for wrought plate, two quite different and distinctive marks replaced the leopard's head and the lion. They were the "figure of a woman commonly called Britannia" and a lion's head erased (showing the neck jagged, as if it had been torn off). A new series of date letters was introduced from the enforcement of the Act on March 25, 1697. Because the goldsmiths customarily changed the letter at the end of May, the second letter of the new series commenced on May 30, 1697. The Britannia standard remained enforced until June 1, 1720. On the restoration of the optional sterling standard, no change of date letter was made, the series continuing with 'E' for 1720–1721. Some makers continued to work with the Britannia standard, especially for important pieces – notably Paul De Lamerie, who did not turn to sterling until 1732. The Britannia standard, though condemned to abolition by the recommendations of the Departmental Committee on Hallmarking in 1959, is still legal and sometimes used; it is, of course, marked with the Britannia and lion's head erased instead of the leopard's head and lion passant marks.

Figure of Britannia seated
with lion's head erased

The Act of 1696, aimed primarily at protecting the coinage, which was being melted down on a large scale to supply an apparently insatiable demand for plate, ignored the provincial silversmiths. In 1700, therefore, the Plate Assay Act named the assay offices in York, Exeter, Bristol, Chester and Norwich, being towns where Mints had been "lately erected for recoining the money of the Kingdom". Newcastle-upon-Tyne was omitted, and had to wait until 1702 for reinstatement. The Statutes of 1700 and 1702 were important not only in their laying down regulations for the assay offices but for their virtual regulation of the trade, incorporating as separate companies "the goldsmiths, silversmiths and plateworkers who are or shall be freemen of and inhabiting within any of the said Cities and having served an apprenticeship to the said trade".

The chequered history of provincial silversmithing in the United Kingdom is one of unending fascination. Much has yet to be uncovered and correlated to the work already done. Some provincial work is of a very high order, some is less competent and drags far behind the designs and skills of the London makers. Some provincial towns are represented by only a handful of pieces – Bristol, for instance, although specified as a Mint town in both 1423 and 1700. Some are scarcely recorded – Sherborne in Dorset and Gateshead in County Durham. Some, like Exeter, York and Newcastle had long and distinguished histories in silversmithing, surviving into the nineteenth century. Chester, one of the oldest of all provincial assay offices, closed its doors in 1962, so that the two youngest assay offices, Birmingham and Sheffield, established in 1773, now remain the only English ones outside London.

When in 1719 the Plate Duty Act was framed, imposing a duty of sixpence an ounce on all plate wrought in England and Scotland, the small sop offered to the silversmiths was the restoration of the old sterling standard. Though saving the expense of the finer, high-standard silver, this Act was the first of the many restrictions on the craft which caused the less scrupulous to turn to evasion, and which in the long run resulted in the innumerable anomalies in the hallmarking laws that still beset the trade. Its immediate effect was to introduce the illegal practice of 'duty-dodging'. In 1757 collection of duty had become so difficult that the duty was repealed and replaced by a two-pound licence, due from all those 'trading in, selling or vending Gold or Silver Plate'', which was only repealed in 1949. Taxes on gold and silver have always been a useful source of revenue, however, and in 1784 the government reverted to the old idea of a duty on plate. They ordered sixpence an ounce to be paid at the time of assay, each piece to be stamped with the sovereign's head mark on payment of the duty. The mark, showing the sovereign's head in profile, consequently appeared on all hallmarked silver from December 1, 1784, until the duty was removed on May 1, 1890. On occasion the mark was struck twice – for some nine months from July, 1797, by the Birmingham and Sheffield assay offices, to indicate that the duty was one shilling an ounce in that year.

More recently, the sovereign's head mark was used with happier association. A touch showing the heads in profile of King George V and Queen Mary was used from 1933 until 1936 to celebrate their Silver Jubilee in 1935, and Queen Elizabeth's coronation was commemorated by her head shown in profile in 1952 and 1953.

In studying hallmarks on silver notice has to be taken not only of the marks themselves but also of the outlines and the shields in which they are contained. Each series of date letters, for instance, is either characteristically different from its predecessors, or is used in association with different marks. At first glance, the cycles starting in 1776 and 1816 in London, both using small Roman letters in shields with cut corners and points at the base, are alike. But in 1776 the leopard's head was still a majestic beast wearing a crown, and by the time the 1816 cycle began, there was no fear of confusion, because George III's head had taken its place with the other marks. Moreover, when the letter 'l' for 1826 was reached, the first year in which confusion might have arisen again, the leopard had become a catlike animal without a crown.

London Marks*

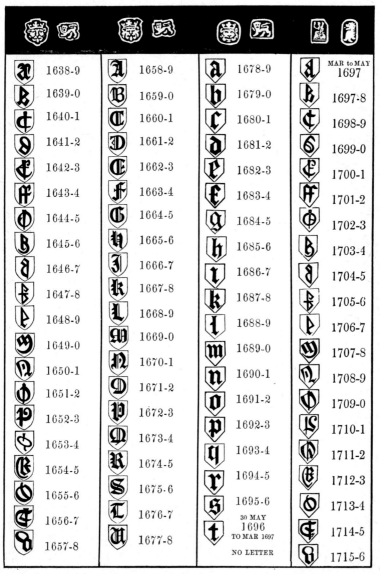

𝔞	1638-9	𝔄	1658-9	𝔞	1678-9	𝔄	MAR to MAY 1697
𝔟	1639-0	𝔅	1659-0	𝔟	1679-0	𝔟	1697-8
𝔠	1640-1	ℭ	1660-1	𝔠	1680-1	𝔠	1698-9
𝔡	1641-2	𝔇	1661-2	𝔡	1681-2	𝔇	1699-0
𝔢	1642-3	𝔈	1662-3	𝔢	1682-3	𝔈	1700-1
𝔣	1643-4	𝔉	1663-4	𝔣	1683-4	𝔉	1701-2
𝔤	1644-5	𝔊	1664-5	𝔤	1684-5	𝔤	1702-3
𝔥	1645-6	𝔥	1665-6	𝔥	1685-6	𝔥	1703-4
𝔦	1646-7	𝔍	1666-7	𝔦	1686-7	𝔦	1704-5
𝔨	1647-8	𝔎	1667-8	𝔨	1687-8	𝔨	1705-6
𝔩	1648-9	𝔏	1668-9	𝔩	1688-9	𝔩	1706-7
𝔪	1649-0	𝔐	1669-0	𝔪	1689-0	𝔪	1707-8
𝔫	1650-1	𝔑	1670-1	𝔫	1690-1	𝔫	1708-9
𝔬	1651-2	𝔒	1671-2	𝔬	1691-2	𝔒	1709-0
𝔭	1652-3	𝔓	1672-3	𝔭	1692-3	𝔭	1710-1
𝔮	1653-4	𝔔	1673-4	𝔮	1693-4	𝔔	1711-2
𝔯	1654-5	𝔕	1674-5	𝔯	1694-5	𝔕	1712-3
𝔰	1655-6	𝔖	1675-6	𝔰	1695-6	𝔰	1713-4
𝔱	1656-7	𝔗	1676-7	𝔱	30 MAY 1696 TO MAR 1697 NO LETTER	𝔗	1714-5
𝔲	1657-8	𝔘	1677-8			𝔘	1715-6

*This is the complete list from 1638 to 1964 of the London date letters; full cycles existed before, but the great periods of silver followed the Restoration. At the head of each column are the appropriate standard and London assay-office marks which changed with each new cycle.

A	1716-7	**a**	1736-7	**A**	1756-7	**a**	1776-7
B	1717-8	**b**	1737-8	**B**	1757-8	**b**	1777-8
C	1718-9	**c**	1738-9	**C**	1758-9	**c**	1778-9
D	1719-0	**d**	1739-0	**D**	1759-0	**d**	1779-0
E	1720-1	**e**	1740-1	**E**	1760-1	**e**	1780-1
F	1721-2	**f**	1741-2	**F**	1761-2	**f**	1781-2
G	1722-3	**g**	1742-3	**G**	1762-3	**g**	1782-3
H	1723-4	**h**	1743-4	**H**	1763-4	**h**	1783-4
I	1724-5	**i**	1744-5	**J**	1764-5	**i**	1784-5
K	1725-6	**k**	1745-6	**K**	1765-6	**k**	1785-6
L	1726-7	**l**	1746-7	**L**	1766-7	**l**	1786-7
M	1727-8	**m**	1747-8	**M**	1767-8	**m**	1787-8
N	1728-9	**n**	1748-9	**N**	1768-9	**n**	1788-9
O	1729-0	**o**	1749-0	**O**	1769-0	**o**	1789-0
P	1730-1	**p**	1750-1	**P**	1770-1	**p**	1790-1
Q	1731-2	**q**	1751-2	**Q**	1771-2	**q**	1791-2
R	1732-3	**r**	1752-3	**R**	1772-3	**r**	1792-3
S	1733-4	**f**	1753-4	**S**	1773-4	**s**	1793-4
T	1734-5	**t**	1754-5	**T**	1774-5	**t**	1794-5
V	1735-6	**u**	1755-6	**U**	1775-6	**u**	1795-6

a. from June, 1720   b. from 1786

74

London Marks

A	1796-7	a	1816-7	A	1836-7	a	1856-7
B	1797-8	b	1817-8	B	1837-8	b	1857-8
C	1798-9	c	1818-9	C	1838-9	c	1858-9
D	1799-0	d	1819-0	D	1839-0	d	1859-0
E	1800-1	e	1820-1	E	1840-1	e	1860-1
F	1801-2	f	1821-2	F	1841-2	f	1861-2
G	1802-3	g	1822-3	G	1842-3	g	1862-3
H	1803-4	h	1823-4	H	1843-4	h	1863-4
I	1804-5	i	1824-5	J	1844-5	i	1864-5
K	1805-6	k	1825-6	K	1845-6	k	1865-6
L	1806-7	l	1826-7	L	1846-7	l	1866-7
M	1807-8	m	1827-8	M	1847-8	m	1867-8
N	1808-9	n	1828-9	N	1848-9	n	1868-9
O	1809-0	o	1829-0	O	1849-0	o	1869-0
P	1810-1	p	1830-1	P	1850-1	p	1870-1
Q	1811-2	q	1831-2	Q	1851-2	q	1871-2
R	1812-3	r	1832-3	R	1852-3	r	1872-3
S	1813-4	s	1833-4	S	1853-4	s	1873-4
T	1814-5	t	1834-5	T	1854-5	t	1874-5
U	1815-6	u	1835-6	U	1855-6	u	1875-6

c. from 1821   d. from 1837

	1876-7		1896-7		1916-7		1936-7
A	1877-8	a	1897-8	a	1917-8	A	1937-8
B	1878-9	b	1898-9	b	1918-9	B	1938-9
C	1879-0	c	1899-0	c	1919-0	C	1939-0
D	1880-1	d	1900-1	d	1920-1	D	1940-1
E	1881-2	e	1901-2	e	1921-2	E	1941-2
F	1882-3	f	1902-3	f	1922-3	F	1942-3
G	1883-4	g	1903-4	g	1923-4	G	1943-4
H	1884-5	h	1904-5	h	1924-5	H	1944-5
I	1885-6	i	1905-6	i	1925-6	I	1945-6
K	1886-7	k	1906-7	k	1926-7	K	1946-7
L	1887-8	l	1907-8	l	1927-8	L	1947-8
M	1888-9	m	1908-9	m	1928-9	M	1948-9
N	1889-0	n	1909-0	n	1929-0	N	1949-0
O	1890-1	o	1910-1	o	1930-1	O	1950-1
P	1891-2	p	1911-2	p	1931-2	P	1951-2
Q	1892-3	q	1912-3	q	1932-3	Q	1952-3
R	1893-4	r	1913-4	r	1933-4	R	1953-4
S	1894-5	s	1914-5	s	1934-5	S	1954-5
T	1895-6	t	1915-6	t	1935-6	T	1955-6
U		u		u		U	

(letter rows A–U correspond to the dates as shown above)

e. Queen Victoria duty mark to 1890

f. Jubilee mark 1933-5

g. Coronation mark 1952-3

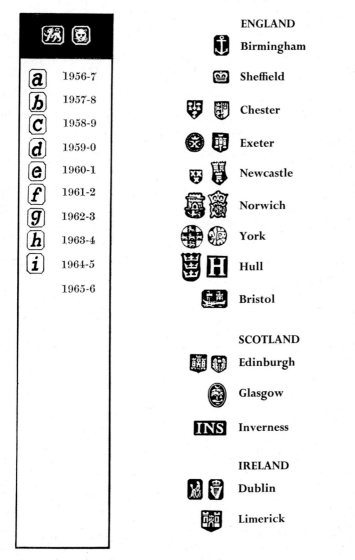

a	1956-7
b	1957-8
c	1958-9
d	1959-0
e	1960-1
f	1961-2
g	1962-3
h	1963-4
i	1964-5
	1965-6

ENGLAND

Birmingham

Sheffield

Chester

Exeter

Newcastle

Norwich

York

Hull

Bristol

SCOTLAND

Edinburgh

Glasgow

Inverness

IRELAND

Dublin

Limerick

Assessing the Hallmarks

Worn marks and partly-marked or unmarked pieces can prove a headache to the collector. Worn marks may be the scheming snare of some faker, or they may indeed be the result of years of wear and tear and hard rubbing by over-zealous polishers. Unmarked pieces may be unmarked treasures, and it is up to the collector to decide their worth. There is no doubt that many pieces of good and even of most excellent silver were, for some reason or another, through intent or by misunderstanding of the law, left unmarked. It is not unusual to find pieces made for royal presentation in the late seventeenth and early eighteenth century unmarked, or bearing the maker's mark only. The excuse for not marking is that the wares were never "set to sale". In the provinces, where assay offices were few and authorities capable of testing and marking silver even fewer, the maker probably as often as not took it upon himself to guarantee his metal simply by his own mark. The question of worn marks being frauds evokes the whole problem of fakes and forgeries.

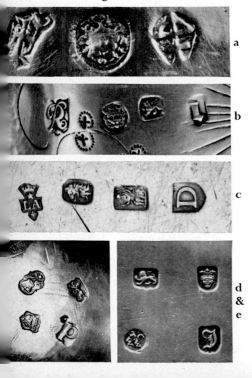

a

A tea caddy showing how a faker has inserted a disc bearing the hallmarks for 1769, and soldered it between the foot and the body.

▶

b

◀

LONDON MARKS

a. Date letter F for 1503. Leopard's head crowned. Crossbow maker's mark.

c

b. Maker's mark PR in monogram. Leopard's head crowned. Lion passant sterling mark. i for 1686.

c. LA for Paul De Lamerie. Lion's head erased. Britannia mark. D for 1719.

d
&
e

d. PL crowned for Paul De Lamerie. Leopard's head crowned. Lion passant sterling mark. d for 1739.

e. TW CW for Thomas Whipham and Charles Wright. Lion passant. Leopard's head. I for 1764.

Fakes and Forgeries

Fakes and forgeries of silver are not a phenomenon of modern times; when the mediaeval hallmarking laws were framed, fakers of silver had been at their unpleasant trade for thousands of years. There are ancient Roman forgeries of Greek treasures, there are Roman silver fakes, and the scant records of gold-smithing in early England are full of complaints about sub-standard and plated metal.

There are four main kinds of hallmarking offence: the transposition of marks from one piece to another; the actual forging of punches; the copying of genuine pieces by casting or electrotyping; and illegal alterations or additions to a hallmarked piece.

The transposition of marks is probably the most commonly committed of all hallmarking offences. It was a practice among less scrupulous silversmiths during the onerous years of the sixpence per ounce duty between 1719 and 1758 to evade the tax by what has come to be known as 'duty-dodging'. The

usual method was for a genuine set of hallmarks, perhaps from a small or a damaged piece, to be cut out and soldered carefully into position in a new, large piece on which the duty would be formidable. It was even worth sending a small article, such as a caster or small dish, weighing a few ounces, to be assayed and marked in the proper way. The marks could then be cut out and the disc soldered in place in the base of the large new piece. The simplest place to let in the marks would be between the body and the foot, where the extra solder needed would be scarcely noticeable. But sometimes the silversmiths, who were fully aware of the usual position in which the Assay Master placed the marks, would find it advisable to follow current practice. On a jug or a tankard for instance, he would have to conceal his patch near the handle, hiding the solder-line by overlapping decoration at that point. By careful scrutiny, the thin line of solder can sometimes be detected, and breathing on the surface around the hallmark will often reveal the edge of the insertion

Fine chocolate-pot and stand, teapot and stand and tea-kettle with lamp and stand, made by Joseph Ward in 1719. The kettle is, in fact, a 'duty dodger', the maker having avoided paying duty on the 85-ounce kettle by transposing a mark from some other ware.

Similar methods of transposing hallmarks have been used by later fakers than the duty-dodgers whose aim was merely to evade duty. When collecting old silver became fashionable in the late nineteenth century, there were plenty of rogues ready to pass off recently made, often sub-standard wares as genuine antiques. Their undoing is almost always their lack of knowledge. The solder of the past, for instance, was brazed over charcoal and it contained brass, both of which gave it a yellowish colour, whereas modern solder contains whitening zinc.

Stretched, twisted and otherwise distorted marks are another sign of the forger. Apart from badly damaged silver, spoons are the cheapest way of obtaining a collection of antique hallmarks, but spoon stems are thick, and it needs considerable skill – for which the forger is not usually prepared to pay – to convert the slim line of marks into a piece suitable for insertion without stretching them a little or distorting the edges of the shields.

Forging of marks themselves and applying them to wares, often of sub-standard metal, is another method of the faker, and was especially rife in the years at the turn of this century, when antique silver collecting was at an unprecedented peak but when the knowledgeable collector was much rarer than he is today. There has, indeed, been no large-scale forging of marks for more than forty years. Greedy in the hope of quick gain, the forger of marks generally tended to use copper, not steel, for his punches, thereby betraying himself by the rather 'soft' appearance of his marks. These marks are, of course, difficult for the inexperienced to detect, for wear and rubbing over the years often blurs the edges of genuine hallmarks. Makers' marks, for example, are often less strongly impressed than the hallmarks on a genuine piece, and the difference may help to verify authenticity. Also, as suggested above, forgers are not usually very knowledgeable about current practices regarding the position of the marks, and an exceptional placing should immediately make the collector wary.

Cast Forgeries

Partial obliteration of modern marks to make them appear as though they were old worn ones is only feasible with silver marked with the Britannia standard marks – the maker's mark and the date letter are rubbed down almost to extinction in the hope of deceiving the unwary. Pieces so faked are usually, of course, reproductions of early eighteenth-century wares, and the collector here is best safeguarded by his knowledge of manufacturing changes, and the small details that do in fact distinguish modern and antique silver – from the patina earned by age to the fashion in which the solder has been turned away.

Copying of genuine antique silverwares by casting or electrotyping – the latter being very rare indeed – is another form of forgery. The perpetrator's greed is his downfall – presuming a sensible appreciation on the collector's part of the value of hallmark study. A single, early eighteenth-century candlestick is a worthwhile acquisition. A pair is more than twice the value of one, a quartet provides a treasure indeed. The same is true of good sets of early spoons or forks. To forge these wares by casting, however, three aspects become obvious: the marks on the castings are softened in the process; decoration is similarly affected, and cannot appear as sharp as on the original – a factor especially noticeable concerning the ubiquitous crests and coats-of-arms found on early silver. Secondly, flaws on the original must be faithfully reproduced in the casting. It is unlikely that all four hallmarks would be worn in exactly the same way on the base of even two candlesticks, while on a set of spoons the individual application of the punches means that the chances of all the marks on two, four or six spoons being in identical positions are very remote. Thirdly, even wares originally cast were not cast

◀ **Since each mark is applied individually, it is very unlikely that all the marks on one piece would be in identical positions to those on another. Here all three have been cast from an original of 1698.**

in one piece, but were usually built up from several sections and do, of course, show traces of solder at the joints. This is especially true of the late nineteenth-century imitations of apostle spoons and other cast-top spoons.

Alterations and additions to silverwares without submitting them for assay and marking were made illegal by the Gold and Silver Wares Act of 1844. 'Improving' of earlier silver, usually by the addition of chased decoration, but occasionally by more drastic additions or alterations, was a favourite early nineteenth-century trait. Quantities of early eighteenth-century, plain silver have been ruined in the eyes of modern collectors by this addition of rather florid decoration, though these pieces do not break the law. In fact, restoration of these pieces to their pristine state of plainness is also still quite legal under present law. Illegality creeps in when restoration and repair work entail adding new metal or replacing a part. Simple additions, whereby the character or use of the article is unchanged, providing the addition is not as much as one third of the original weight of the piece, are permissible, but they must be sent for assay and marked. The old marks are allowed to remain. Where the addition is more than a third, or the character of the ware is altered, the whole piece must be re-assayed and newly marked.

Alterations with intent to deceive are quite another matter. Some of these forgeries are quite ridiculous. The case of a Tudor communion cup inverted and provided with a handle, cover and spout to make a coffee pot is unlikely to deceive even the greenest collector. There are, however, limitless types of alteration, many of them misleading unless proper account is taken of style and form. Mugs and tankards are sometimes found converted into more saleable jugs, or a large sugar basin or slop bowl turned into a feasible sort of teapot. Often such pieces can quite simply be rectified, although their value as antiques must be diminished by the restoration and re-marking of the parts.

Modern forgers have a grasping liking for converting trifid

spoons into the much rarer and therefore much more expensive forks of the period, while meat dishes are sometimes encountered that have been stretched out from worn dinner plates – incidentally stretching the hallmark at the same time. During the early years of this century, the great 'lighthouse' casters, so favoured

This was, in fact, never designed to be a teapot except by someone who decided to transform an old Dublin sugar basin of 1808!

by collectors, were also favoured with the attention of the faker, and plain tankards grew into vast – and improperly marked – casters to lure the unwary. Illegal additions are also sometimes made to wares that have been 'restored' to their original form. The removal of chasing may, for instance, weaken the sides of a piece and the restorer will repair the damage by adding a thin plate to strengthen the walls, probably covering his repair up by plating it over. The pure silver used in plating has not, of course, the same colour or patina as old sterling or Britannia standard silvers, and any suspected conversion or restored piece should be carefully inspected for traces of plating.

The advent of Sheffield plate and, some eighty years later, of electroplating, at first caused qualms among the silversmiths and the authorities, just as, in fact, gilding had done centuries before.

Sheffield plate, which has become a collector's subject in its own right, had its heyday between 1760 and 1850, a period almost exactly coincident with the Soho factory in Birmingham of Matthew Boulton and with the rise of the silver and the plating trades in Sheffield. The importance of Sheffield plate is that the layer of silver is silver of the sterling standard, which is fused on to a copper core. In early work, the thickness of silver was relatively great, though this was reduced considerably about 1810 when the method of rubbing in silver shields solved the problem of engraving armorials without revealing the copper below. Much Sheffield plate was of a high order of workmanship, with designs very akin to those used for silver at the period. Old Sheffield plate, after years of use, does acquire a patina very like that on sterling silver, but also, it should be remembered, the fused coat of silver does tend to wear, and glints of the copper beneath reveal the ware for what it is – quite apart from the maker's marks which, though occasionally similar to, are only imitative of assay marks.

Silver-plated, or more properly, electroplated wares, are given a thin layer of silver which to adhere properly must be 99.99 per cent pure silver. Its bright appearance, so different from the soft grey lustre of well-aged silver, makes confusion with genuine silverwares unlikely, though the use of electroplating to conceal nefarious solder marks or other faults in forged silverwares needs a sharp and a critical eye whenever doubtful pieces are suspected.

It cannot be too strongly stressed that knowledge is the collector's surest safeguard against fakes and forgeries. Collectable silver is not just old silver, hallowed with the patina of age and centuries-old marks. Each piece of silver is part of the history of silversmithing. It was made for a purpose, to be used or displayed. It should bear marks that denote its maker, its standard, and where and when it was made. If it does not, there may be a good reason for that – or even a bad one. If the marks look wrong, or the piece looks wrong, or even some small detail of the piece looks out of character, then the wise collector summons all his knowledge to his aid. He should not be afraid of asking the advice of experts; nor should he be afraid of passing judgment himself. The collector who gets to know silver and to love it will not be taken in by the few fakes that make their way on to the market.

4

COLLECTORS AND COLLECTING

What to collect and how to collect are two problems that beset
the novice collector. The fact that he wants to collect at all is
probably inborn. Most owners of collections either large or
small admit that the habit afflicted them from childhood onwards, bringing down on their heads the irate comments of
adults about their seemingly vast and unnecessary collections of
stamps, postcards, dolls, toy soldiers or the heterogeneous
muddle that goes towards a scrapbook.

Most collectors are in fact born. A lucky few have collections
thrust upon them, but to acquire the stimulus late in life is
rare indeed. A specialised knowledge does not necessarily make
a collector – one of the most informed authorities on silver admits
to having no desire at all to form a collection of it. Yet collectors
who try to rid themselves of the habit seldom succeed. There is
many a story of the collector who decided to dispose of his fine
array of antiques, only to start again the moment the last piece
has left his hands. Indeed, one famous spoon collector was hard
into his third outstanding spoon collection when he died, each
one a fine, carefully chosen and specialised group.

Specialisation in one type of silver is often the choice of the
collector today, especially since early eighteenth-century domestic silver, such as one would most enjoy using in the home, is
rare and expensive. This does not mean that the silver enthusiast
of modest means is precluded from finding good usable domestic

Fine domestic silver is probably the most sought
after of all antique plate. This fine coffee-pot by
Edward Pocock, 1734, with its tapered cylindrical
body on rim foot, graceful swan-neck spout, flat-
domed cover and turned wooden handle, the body
enhanced with a fine engraved coat-of-arms in a
baroque cartouche is the type of silver that is fast
increasing in price.

silver. There are a wide range of pieces, such as small table-salts, milk and cream jugs, sauce-boats, coasters and spoons and forks, as well as some larger wares of the later eighteenth and early nineteenth centuries that come well within his grasp.

One of the joys of studying silver is the variety of things that were made in the beautiful metal. Since the Restoration, almost everything used at table and a good many household effects as well as much for personal use have been made in silver. At one end of the scale there is the now unobtainable and only rarely surviving silver furniture. Then there are massive wine coolers and wine fountains, great chargers, ewers and basins for rose-water, flagons and table centres. At the other end, there are little things made in silver for those who could not afford gold about their person – snuff and tobacco boxes, for instance, patch boxes and vinaigrettes. Since mediaeval times, most households had at least a silver spoon for each member, and perhaps also a tankard and a beaker. Aside from references in wills and inventories, there is the confirmation of the finds of silver buried in the seventeenth century by Danish tenant farmers fleeing from invaders and the strife of civil wars: most caches included one or two beakers, a tankard or large cup and anything up to a dozen spoons. There seems no reason to expect anything different in England. And for the modern collector, spoons have provided a plentiful and a fascinating subject of study.

Nowadays, few people have room enough to store large and unwieldy objects that are not in regular use, so that the demand for domestic silver, especially that for tea and coffee, is always heavy, both at home and abroad. This has led many people to bemoan the shortage of fine silver to be had. It is not, however, so much a shortage as an increased demand that has boosted the price and therefore mantled the silver with a rarity value beyond the purses of many collectors. Today there are, moreover, many collectors with perhaps more refined tastes than those of the great collecting period at the turn of the century. Changed

Not all early silver is prohibitively expensive for the novice collector, and there are many interesting and useful examples of flatware to intrigue and delight him. *From top to bottom:* A cheese scoop, made in Birmingham in 1827; a good heavy gauge marrow scoop by E. Cathcart, London, 1752; a fancy back strainer spoon of about 1750; an apple corer with small spice caster in the end, about 1690.

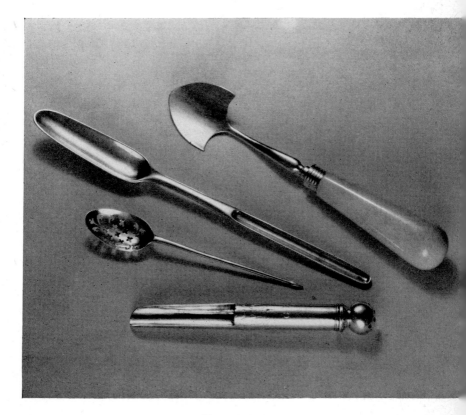

tastes have changed demand for certain types of silver. Collectors nowadays tend to leave Tudor and early Stuart silver to the museums, not because it is rare and expensive but because it is less in accord with their tastes today.

Knowledge of a particular subject often leads to special collections. A doctor, for example, may find himself intrigued by the multifarious surgical and other medical instruments which probably go unrecognised as oddities by the general collector. Until the development of stainless steel, most instruments were of silver or gold, and there are many ancillary items such as tongue scrapers, tongue depressors and medicine spoons. Those interested in gaming may find great pleasure in the silver counters and other pieces connected with such pastimes. For the sportsman there are many interesting trophies, a great many of them far less mundane than the ubiquitous silver cups and medals of today. In the seventeenth century, for instance, porringers, thistle cups and swords all featured as race prizes, while the next hundred years saw punch bowls, tumbler cups, and even coffeepots on the racecourse. Even the nineteenth-century sportsman was not always restricted to cups, and silver churchwarden pipes, bugles, a silver fishing-reel and silver dog-collars made appropriate items.

There is no end to the variety of subjects that the silver collector can use to interesting advantage. The man who has travelled or lived in the East may perhaps like to collect pieces with an eastern flavour – perhaps the early so-called 'Buddha knop' spoons, or silver decorated in the Chinese taste, or that made abroad for British colonials. The housewife collector can find enjoyment in kitchen pieces, from great preserving pans to small saucepans for warming brandy or sauce – or, more likely, cream which was warmed to take in tea in the early part of the eighteenth century. There are, too, rarities such as cream skimmers and pie dishes in silver, as well as small pieces such as apple-corers, nutmeg-graters, wine-funnels and ladles.

The Search for Silver

Sometimes subjects overlap. The wine enthusiast looking for wine tasters, strainers, funnels and the like may have to vie with the collector of kitchen wares or the wine-label specialist; the social historian looking for pocket nutmeg-graters may find himself up against the collector who chooses those things to do with punch-making, though if he searches hard enough he may find objects unrecorded or unknown, that have somehow or other escaped a dusty death in an old attic or butler's pantry – such as the little adjustable frame and shade which helped to prevent a candle from blowing out; it came from an Irish house noted for its draughtiness.

Sometimes dating of provincial silver can only be approximate; styles are often a little curious, and rarity sends prices soaring. This small Newcastle porringer, made about 1675, is probably by William Ramsay. The maker's mark WR is used with the rose mark associated with Ramsay, but there is no town mark or date letter.

Pieces with inscriptions make a fascinating study. Not all inscriptions are contemporary with the piece, nor are all by any means important, either historically or as works of art. Some are just charming tokens of affection or esteem; some record events or societies which must send the collector to pore over books and other records to build up the story that enhances the piece. Occasionally the collector of historical silver has his find enriched by documentary or other evidence: for example, a cup of 1792, made by Pitts & Preedy of London, was given by the Prince of Wales, later George IV, to a certain Captain Burton for having preserved the life of Countess Noel (the *Duchesse de Noailles*) by bringing her, dressed as a boy and concealed in his ship, from France to Brighton. The cup is accompanied by a watercolour portrait of Captain Burton, a properly dour man of whose integrity the Prince can surely have had no qualms.

Provincial silver attracts many different types of silver collector. The hallmarks enthusiast finds in it a splendid variety of marks. The collector concentrating on early pieces usually has a choice between London spoons and provincial pieces. For the student of unmarked or partly marked silver, there is plenty attributable to the provincial centres, while a man living in the country is often in a position to find locally made and marked pieces to help his collection along. For the research worker, too, provincial silver offers an as yet far from exhausted study. There are enthusiasts working in different part of the country, accumulating and assimilating the scanty knowledge of provincial assay offices and silversmiths, though their work is relatively only beginning. Much still needs to be done, especially in the light of recent discoveries.

In the last twenty-five years, there has been an increase in the study of silver and silversmiths. Some has been published, some is still in the process of being worked out. Some old theories and often repeated dicta have been discarded, but researchers must still accord many thanks to the indefatigable

Captain Burton's Cup. ▶

(though sometimes a little misguided) gentlemen who worked so hard and wrote so much in the 1880's and later.

Keeping up with new discoveries about makers and marks is a heavy but a very rewarding task, and one that adds infinitely to the pleasure of old silver. The collector needs to have a good and a reliable memory for marks and for forms and styles. Even if his particular interests do not extend to the whole field of English silver, he should at least be conversant with pieces outside his own sphere, and, indeed, outside the world of silver altogether. Each piece is a reflection of its age, of the skill of its maker and the taste of the patrons of the period. Silver, no more than any other craft, deserves proper study, not relegation to a vacuum. There are, for example, many interesting parallels to be drawn with other arts and crafts, especially pottery and porcelain, furniture and architecture. More than one craftsman trained in silver has made his name outside his trade – Hogarth turned to painting and engraving; Nicholas Sprimont was the first manager of the Chelsea porcelain factory; and in reverse, masters of other crafts, such as Robert Adam, John Flaxman and C. H. Tatham had extensive influence on the work of silversmiths. Comparison with Continental and other silver work makes a useful study, especially in judging how much overseas influence and interchange of design ideas obtained at any special period. Painting and literature likewise can furnish the collector with information that helps to bring silver into perspective in the history of English art.

Collecting scraps of information, photographs and illustrations of different pieces, great or small, museum and saleroom catalogues, magazine articles and dealers' advertisements in the weekly and monthly magazines can all help to build up the ordered history of silversmithing in England in the collector's mind. With practice he should at a glance be able to distinguish the approximate date of a piece of silver. Knowing silver in this way is very helpful in dealing with unmarked silver. Indeed, to pick up a piece and attribute it to a place and date, possibly even a maker as well, is useful and stimulating practice. This should always be done before looking for the hallmarks, and, if there is none there, then at least the piece has been assessed on its intrinsic qualities first of all. Dating a piece on its appearance is not so difficult as it may sound. The pace of change in silver design has always been slow, and changes, when they have come, have always been clearly perceptible and datable.

To handle silver often is, of course, a vital part of learning about it. The feel of silver is somehow almost as critical as its appearance. There is no point, unless to collect a rare mark, in buying flimsy or badly designed silver. A broken piece that cannot be satisfactorily mended without additions (and therefore later hallmarking) is virtually valueless, whatever its marks Silver is meant to be used, not kept in a glass cage, as though too delicate to be handled and enjoyed.

Good silverware is not cheap. The bargains of yesteryear were even then rare, and are rarer still today. Some pieces have rocketed to an unattainable height. Certain makers have acquired a cachet so that their work, however small, insignificant, dull or even excruciatingly ugly, still fetches a high price, while the work of other makers, perhaps just as competent, or even better, is obtainable at more reasonable prices. This has happened to Hester Bateman, especially in the United States, and her mark means high prices even when it appears on very pedestrian wares. So, too, with Paul De Lamerie. Here there is never any doubt about fine workmanship, but at times, especially in his later years, between about 1745 and his death in 1751, his designs could on occasions be quite unattractive. Aesthetics are as important as quality in silver collecting.

Many collectors, especially those starting a collection and particularly those of modest means, are hesitant about asking advice. In later years, they are sometimes surprised to find that other silver collectors, among them the reputable silver dealers, are more than ready to talk about silver at almost any time of the day or night. A good dealer is a good friend. He will advise, he will seek out the sort of silver that suits the collector and, while no one would expect him to work for nothing, his prices are often very reasonable and the time he spends looking out for pieces, his advice and knowledge are often invaluable and worth more than his percentage of profit.

A variety of moderately priced pieces include a sugar basket with border of bright-cut engraving by Peter and Ann Bateman, 1797, a teapot made in London in 1814, an early caster, by Thomas Bamford, 1731, and a small sauce boat on three hoof feet made in London in 1764.

Cleaning Silver

Tarnish on silver is caused by sulphur in the atmosphere combining with the silver itself and forming silver sulphide. The thicker the layer of tarnish, the more purplish black the layer of corroding chemical becomes, until removal can only be effected by drastic methods best undertaken by the professional.

Tarnish is best countered by using silver, washing it regularly and polishing it gently with a soft cloth. Silver left stored in cupboards or drawers usually gets much more tarnished than everyday silver, though in smoky towns, of course, the burning of coal, gas and oil all increase the sulphur content of the air and aggravate tarnishing processes.

Silver takes a good polish, but all polishing has the effect of removing metal in the process. After many years this becomes appreciable, and it may also have the sad result of obliterating details of decoration, engraving and, of course, the hallmarks. It is a good idea to keep one's thumb over the marks during cleaning.

From time to time, however, all silver needs polishing to bring up its fine lustre. Rouge requires some skill in use, and though for the professional silversmith it is undoubtedly still the best polish available, in the home it is messy and difficult to use.

It was in 1839 that a Midlands chemist, Joseph Goddard, took the first commercial step in producing a safe and simple plate polish, which was non-mercurial. Plate powders of the type he invented, plus the more convenient, liquid plate polishes and creams, remain the basic silver-cleaning equipment of many homes; indeed, it took more than a century before Goddard's own descendants brought out the revolutionary dip methods of cleaning plate. These have certain special advantages, in that they remove even well-established tarnish quickly and easily, though they do need polishing after drying.

Most polishes now contain some form of protective coating that helps to keep the silver bright for much longer than previously, thus cutting down the need for cleaning to only three or four times a year. One of the newest and cleanest methods for the user is the foaming polish, which is applied with a damp sponge and at once lathers and attacks the tarnish. Its action is eminently gentle, and black clothes and dirty hands are avoided, the lather and tarnish being rinsed off together in warm water.

Impregnated cotton polishing-cloths and a good soft chamois leather help to maintain the polish and lustre of silver between regular cleaning sessions. Brushes for penetrating crevices and chasing should be of good quality, soft bristle, and for little-used silver, storage bags, nowadays treated to resist tarnish, and special tissue papers are available.

Of the products which form a protective layer the main ones are rhodium (of the platinum group) which forms an untarnishable, but rather bright plating on the silver, and silicone which is effective for three to four years and which can have ordinary polishes applied on top.

Meanwhile, scientists continue to work on the problems of producing a silver that is tarnish-resistant without lowering the standard from the durable and beautiful sterling. Until that day those who love to use and handle silver will hardly begrudge the few hours that must be spent to keep it as fresh and gleaming as it was when it first emerged from the workshop.

5

MUSEUMS
AND COLLECTIONS

Museums have been called a by-product of the international fairs of the middle of the nineteenth century. Britain's most important collection of the applied arts of recent times – the Victoria & Albert Museum – was mooted as early as 1835, but its final establishment was not until a year after the first Great Exhibition of 1851. Today, museums all over the world are storehouses of knowledge, both specialised and general, sometimes nationally owned, sometimes privately by individuals or societies.

Museums vary much from town to town and country to country. Not all are well endowed. Some have incomes so limited that they are almost entirely dependent on the generosity (always well-meaning but not always entirely suitable for museum display) of private collectors. Others are enriched with exceptional collections bequeathed by eminent collectors. Some are excellently planned, some are sadly deficient in display, designation and information. But all, large or small, private or public, have something to offer to the enquiring collector, and most museum curators are happy to answer serious questions about their exhibits.

In England, the Victoria & Albert Museum contains probably the most representative collection of English silver in the country. It is, of course, the National Collection, and new acquisitions are not infrequently made, many through legacies or with the assistance of the National Art Collections Fund. A

CARL A. RUDISILL LIBRARY
LENOIR RHYNE COLLEGE

most useful series of picture books is available at very moderate cost, illustrating silverwares from the mediaeval period to the reign of Queen Victoria. In addition, exhibitions including silver from private and other collections are often mounted at the Museum.

The Elizabethan Cottonian collection and that of the physician, Hans Sloane, resulted in the formation of the oldest and largest of the museums of Britain, the British Museum, which was opened to the public in 1759. So far as the study of silver goes, the British Museum collection is much more limited than that at the Victoria & Albert, but it provides a useful guide to pre-Commonwealth goldsmithing. The collection chiefly comprises mediaeval and Tudor drinking vessels, the bequest of Sir Wollaston Franks.

Other London museums with displays of silver – and of furniture and other works of art which have a bearing on the study of silver – include the Wallace Collection at Hertford House, the London Museum, and Apsley House, home of the Duke of Wellington and a fine showplace of Regency plate.

Outside London, the Ashmolean Museum at Oxford, with its incomparable collections of Huguenot and rococo plate, acquired through the generosity of W. F. Farrer and A. T. Carter among others, must rank among the finest for silver anywhere in the world. Cardiff (where the National Museum of Wales houses the collection formed by Sir Charles Jackson, the leading authority on English silversmithing of his period), the Royal Scottish Museum at Edinburgh, the Holburne of Menstrie Museum at Bath, and the City Art Gallery and Museum at Birmingham are all deserving of proper study by the silver collector, who would also be well advised to visit the annual Regency exhibition at the Prince Regent's Pavilion at Brighton, the Adam splendour of Temple Newsam House at Leeds and the Burrell Collection in Glasgow. Indeed, every museum has some worthwhile treasure to offer – there is silver at the Fitzwilliam in Cambridge, there is silver to be compared with Sheffield Plate at the City Museum in Sheffield's Weston Park; Manchester and Plymouth, Norwich and Newcastle, Hereford and York, and a dozen or more others can all make their contribution to the study of silversmithing.

Outside England, the attraction of English silver has built up a number of notable collections, especially in the United States of America. Here and there, European collections include English pieces. Of these, the most outstanding is that in the Kremlin, where silverwares have escaped the melting pots of the centuries to provide a collection, unparalleled elsewhere, of Tudor and early Stuart pieces. Occasional English silverwares are to be found in other countries, and one comes upon them perhaps a little surprised: in the National Museum in Stockholm, for instance, the main aisle in the silver section is dominated by a magnificent London-made épergne of 1765, a rare example of the partnership between David Whyte and William Holmes.

In America, the avoidance of heavy duties by presenting treasures to national and state collections has endowed several museums with excellent groups of English silverware. The Sterling and Francine Clark Art Institute in Williamstown, Massachusetts, can boast some thousand examples of English silver. At The Minneapolis Institute of Arts is housed one of the London auction records – the famous Sutherland wine cistern by Paul De Lamerie, to mention but one piece from a fine collection. The assembly of mugs at the Huntington Library and Art Gallery, San Marino, California, is that collected by Mr. and Mrs. W. B. Munro; there are more examples of English silver at the Los Angeles County Museum of Art, at the Fogg Art Museum in Cambridge, Massachusetts, at the Metropolitan Museum of Art, New York, the Philadelphia Museum of Art and the Museum of Fine Arts, Boston, to name but a few. For the traveller in the United States, there are many stopping-off points at which he can broaden his knowledge of English silver.

Fortunately for the silver collector, the museums have not swallowed up all the best of English silver. At present, their collections are designed to awaken public interest in the history of the craft. Outside the museums, there are still a large number of private collections, small and large. In many, now open to the public, the silver can be seen and enjoyed by an ever-growing public. Sometimes these splendid houses and their contents are in the care of trusts, either museums or local or national societies for the preservation of fine things. Mention has been made of Temple Newsam, now in the care of the Corporation of Leeds; Apsley House, London, is now administered by the Victoria & Albert Museum; the Regency Pavilion at Brighton is another. Up and down the country local authorities and private families have opened up houses to public viewing, giving the silver and other treasures a pleasant domestic setting that helps to put the works of art into a period perspective.

Not all collections, of course, are open to the public, and some owners are naturally (and wisely) reticent about their treasures. But most are happy enough to lend them from time to time for exhibition, and in the past sixty years or so there have been a number of exceptional and comprehensive exhibitions of silver in England and elsewhere. Students will often find reference to the exhibitions at the Fitzwilliam Museum in 1895, the Burlington Fine Arts Club in 1901 and 1903, and to the Seaford House and Park Lane Exhibitions in London in 1929. More recently, the Worshipful Company of Goldsmiths has been responsible for exhibitions of silver, old and modern, at their Hall in the City of London, and the catalogues issued are useful data in the study of English silver. In 1951 both modern silver and 'Historic Plate of the City of London' were exhibited, with Corporation Plate from England and Wales the following year, treasures from Oxford in 1953 and from Cambridge in 1959. Royal plate from Windsor and Buckingham Palace was shown at the Victoria & Albert Museum in 1954. Abroad, comprehensive exhibitions in recent years have included:– 'English Silver, 1660–1830' at the National Museum, Stockholm in 1958, 'Old English and Early American Silverwork' at the Los Angeles County Museum of Art in 1962, various group exhibitions since 1953 at the Sterling and Francine Clark Art Institute, and one of English silver in Toronto in 1958.

City Corporations, Boroughs and Colleges, as well as the old-established City Livery Companies, regiments and churches possess much fine plate, and along with modern industrial concerns, are among the most generous of modern patrons of the silversmith. Their collections are, on the whole, likely to remain collections, and are rarely dispersed.

The dispersal of fine collections of silver, sad though it may seem, does afford the collector and the student of silver an opportunity to buy and study treasures that may have been in the possession of a single family for generations. The salerooms and antique silver dealers' shops are in many ways as important a source of knowledge as the museums. Indeed, for the collector, they must often be more important, for they provide an opportunity to examine and handle silver, not often permitted in museums and other collections. It is, of course, an opportunity fraught with the danger that the collector and his money will soon be parted, but it is a danger allayed by the delight of acquiring fine silver to be used and admired and the contentment of "a handsome cupboard of plate".

6

GLOSSARY—BIBLIOGRAPHY

ACANTHUS Conventionalised leaf-decoration based on the plant known as brank-ursine and used on Corinthian capitals. Adapted as chased decoration for silver, especially in the second half of the seventeenth century and in the Adam and Regency periods.

AMORINO A cupid.

ANNEALING Softening and toughening metal by heating and cooling it during hammering or drawing processes, which make it brittle.

ANTHEMION Stylised flower motif based on the honeysuckle of classical Greek ornament. Also sometimes applied to the similar classical decoration known as palmette, derived from the date palm, and much used on silver especially during the late eighteenth century and early nineteenth century.

ARABESQUE Scrolling pattern of leaves and branches.

ARGYLE A spouted jug or pot for gravy, with an inner lining for hot water or a central section for a heated billet; said to have been devised by the fourth Duke of Argyll who objected to cold gravy. Argyles were commonly made between about 1770 and 1820.

ARMORIALS Applied to heraldic insignia or other devices, originally borne on shields by knights and barons to distinguish them; later applied more generally, and frequently used on silver to denote ownership.

Glossary

BALUSTER Curved form, slender above and bulging out below; much used as a stem form for cups and also used for candlesticks, jugs and finials.

BAROQUE The bold, rather naturalistic style prevalent in the late seventeenth century.

BIGGIN A kind of coffee-pot with a strainer, so called after the inventor. Made from about 1795 onwards.

BOUGE (also booge) The shaped part between the bottom and rim of a dish or plate.

BRIGHT-CUT A type of engraving with a distinctively bright appearance due to the back edge of the graver being highly polished, thus burnishing the cut made by the tool. Especially popular in the last quarter of the eighteenth century.

BRITANNIA METAL A mixture of tin, copper and regulus of antimony giving a white, but rather tinny metal, usually electroplated. Introduced about 1770, it is sometimes known as Vickers metal. Not to be confused with Britannia standard silver.

BRITANNIA STANDARD The higher standard for wrought plate, obligatory from March, 1697, until the end of May, 1720, to prevent the conversion of sterling coinage to plate. It contains 958 parts per 1000 pure silver (11 oz. 12 dwts. to the pound Troy) which is 8 dwts. to the pound finer than the 925 sterling standard. Britannia standard silver remained permissible after 1720, and is still sometimes used. The higher standard is indicated by a figure of Britannia seated and a lion's head erased instead of the leopard's head and lion passant marks.

CARTOUCHE An ornament, originally a scroll of paper, adapted for use by engravers to enclose coats-of-arms or other designs.

CARYATID A female figure used as a column or support; also applied to the female figure motifs used as handles on mid-seventeenth century silver.

CAUDLE A hot spiced drink made of oatmeal gruel flavoured with wine or ale, sugar and spice, advocated as a cure for minor ailments during the seventeenth century. Two-handled cups of the period are sometimes called caudle cups. (See also posset.)

CAULKING (also corking) The process during raising in which the top edge of the silverware is hammered back to thicken and strengthen it.

CHINOISERIE Decoration inspired by oriental designs and popular as ornament on silver at three periods. Designs of the earliest period, often very freely interpreted, were either engraved or flat chased and date between about 1680 and 1690; this was followed by a short period when chinoiserie-decorated wares, especially for tea-table silver, were made with Chinese motifs chased in high relief, about 1700. The second fashion for chinoiseries was about 1750, with chasing and piercing executed in the Chinese taste on caddies, tea-pots, épergnes and so on. There was a revival of chinoiserie from about 1810 to 1820.

CUT-CARD Pieces of thin silver sheet cut into patterns, often foliate, and soldered on to tankards, bowls, cups, coffee-pots, etc., to provide a decoration in relief. Introduced about 1650, it was greatly elaborated by the Huguenot silversmiths at the end of the century to build up applied ornament in detail and high relief.

DIAPER Pattern of squares or lozenges, often enclosing flower-heads, dots, and other small motifs.

FESTOON Garland of fruit, flowers or leafage hanging in a curve.

FILIGREE Delicate patterns made by working together fine wires of silver or gold. Caddy spoons of the 1820's and 1830's are sometimes found with filigree insets.

FINIAL Ornament placed on the corner of a pediment or top of a cover.

FLATWARE The generic term for spoons, forks, slices and other canteen wares that have no cutting edge (as opposed to knives, which are cutlery).

FLUTING Channelled decoration, vertical, oblique or sometimes curved, much used in late seventeenth-century silver for stems of candlesticks, on bowls, tankards, etc., and revived during the neo-classical period about 1770.

GADROONING Lobed border composed of stamped or cast convex curves (as opposed to the concave curves of fluting) and arranged vertically or obliquely. Much used for edging in the later seventeenth century, and continuing in use, especially for dishes and plates, throughout the eighteenth and nineteenth centuries.

GROTESQUE Fantastic human or animal forms, often used in conjunction with flowers, foliage and scrolls to produce a bizarre effect.

GUILLOCHE A spiral ornament of two or more ribbons or bands twisted one over another, sometimes enclosing rosettes or wheel-like motifs. Used as a border in sixteenth-century work, and revived during the later neo-classical period at the end of the eighteenth century.

KNOP Small boss or knob, used as a finial, and often in the decorative form of a bud, fruit, etc. Also the protuberant part on the stem of a candlestick, cup, etc.

LAMBREQUIN Decoration with draped or scalloped edge.

MATTING In chasing, the roughened surface produced by punchwork done with a burred tool.

MAZARIN A strainer plate used especially for fish dishes.

MAZER Bowl, cup or other drinking vessel of maple wood mounted with silver. Mostly of mediaeval and Tudor date.

MONTEITH Punch bowl with notched rim, a type popular from about 1680 to 1705. The rim is sometimes removable. Said to have been named after a Scot, called Monteigh, who wore a scalloped cloak.

OVOLO A convex moulding consisting of half-rounds or ovals used as a repeat border, especially in the sixteenth century.

PEG TANKARD Tankard of Scandinavian inspiration, rare in

England, with a row of pegs vertically arranged inside, measuring off the amount each drinker was to take at a time – hence, 'to take down a peg'.

PENNYWEIGHT The twentieth part of an ounce Troy; 'dwt.' is the usual abbreviation.

PILGRIM BOTTLE Large vase-like bottle, copied from the leather bottles carried by travellers in the Middle Ages, and complete with chains by which the bottle could be swished in water to cool the contents. Made in silver in the late seventeenth and early eighteenth century, and occasionally copied in the early nineteenth century.

PLANISHING Smoothing and polishing silver by hammering it with a hammer with a slightly convex polished face.

PLATE Gold and silver wares that have been wrought. The term is less often used today because of the confusion caused by using the word for Sheffield Plate and for electroplated wares.

PLATEAU Large tray or stand, often with mirror centre, used as a table centre, especially during the Regency period.

PORRINGER Two-handled bowl, with or without a cover, and sometimes made with a matching salver. Most common during the second half of the seventeenth century, but also made throughout the eighteenth century. Also often known, in the larger sizes, as a caudle or posset cup. Small, single-handled bowls and those with flat-eared handles were probably also used as porringers for any hot liquid food. Small varieties are commonly termed cupping or bleeding bowls.

POSSET Like caudle, a hot spiced drink of the seventeenth century, and served at country weddings well into the middle years of the eighteenth century. It was hot milk curdled with ale or wine and sweetened and spiced.

POUNCE The powder of gum sandarac (hence, sand) used to smooth the paper after an erasure and prevent the ink from spreading. Small pots or vases with pierced tops were made for inkstands to hold pounce.

Glossary

REEDING A decoration, often used for borders, consisting of narrow, parallel, convex ridges. Sometimes, especially in the second half of the eighteenth century and later, combined with ribbon-like motifs to form reed-and-ribbon borders.

REGENCE The French decorative style typified by delicate strap-work and trelliswork and brought to England at the end of the seventeenth century by the most skilled of the Huguenot refugee silversmiths. The term is not widely used because of possible confusion with our own Regency period at the beginning of the nineteenth century.

ROCOCO Probably derived from the French, *rocaille*, because of the rocky appearance of the decoration; the term rococo was first used (rather scornfully) in the early nineteenth century for the exuberant style of shells, scrolls, asymmetrical forms and fantasy in fashion in England between about 1730 and 1760.

SCONCE Wall light formed of a back plate and branch or branches for candles, and made from the Charles II period onwards. Also formerly used for the candlestick itself and for chamber candlesticks.

SHEFFIELD PLATE Method of fusing a layer of silver to a copper core, invented by Thomas Bolsover of Sheffield about 1743. From about 1765 onwards, much used for candlesticks and many other wares made in imitation of silver. Not made extensively after 1860, when electroplating tended to supersede Sheffield Plate.

SILVER-GILT Silver to which a thin layer of gold has been applied, either for show or as a protection against tarnishing. Until the introduction of electro-gilding in the nineteenth century, gilding was applied by the mercurial method. An amalgam of gold and mercury was pasted on to the area to be gilded, then the mercury driven off by heat. Silver-gilt was often casually known as 'gold' in contrast to 'white', used as a term for silver.

STANDISH Original name for what became the inkstand.

TROY WEIGHT The unit of weight employed by goldsmiths and silversmiths. One pound Troy comprises 12 ounces of 20 pennyweights (dwts.) each. A Troy ounce is equivalent to 1·097 ounces avoirdupois, or 31·1 grammes.

VINAIGRETTE Small box with inner pierced grid for holding an aromatic sponge. Introduced in the mid-eighteenth century and especially popular in the 1830's.

WAITER Small tray, round, square, hexagonal, polygonal, etc., similar in style to the salver and used for handing letters, cups, glasses, etc. Sometimes made *en suite* with the larger salver.

WIRE Metal hammered, cast or drawn into a plain or ornamental rod form and used for decorating or strengthening the edges of cups, bowls, pots, baskets, etc.

BRIEF BIBLIOGRAPHY

1 *STUDIES OF SILVER*
Judith Banister – *An Introduction to Old English Silver* (1965)
J. F. Hayward – *Huguenot Silver in England 1688–1727* (1959)
Sir Charles J. Jackson – *An Illustrated History of English Plate* (two volumes, 1911)
Charles Oman – *English Domestic Silver* (fifth edition, 1962)
Gerald Taylor – *Silver* (1956)
The Connoisseur New Guide to Antique English Silver and Plate(1962)
Victoria & Albert Museum – Small Picture Books (eight on English silver)

2 *HALLMARKS AND MAKERS*
Sir Charles J. Jackson – *English Goldsmiths and Their Marks* (second edition 1921, reprinted 1949)

Bibliography

Frederick Bradbury – *Guide to Marks of Origin on British and Irish Silver Plate* (tenth edition, 1959)
W. Chaffers – *Gilda Aurifabrorum* (1899)
Ambrose Heal – *The London Goldsmiths, 1200–1800* (1935)

3 *JOURNALS*

Antique Collector

Antiques (New York)

Apollo

Collectors' Guide

Connoisseur

Country Life

PART II

*A Historical
Sequence
of
Photographs*

1500–1600

"The chief part likewise of their daily provision is brought in before them (commonly in silver vessels if they be of the degree of barons, bishops or upwards) and placed on their tables. . . . As for drink, it is usually filled in pots, goblets, jugs, bowls of silver . . ."

William Harrison: *Description of England*, 1587.

The great hall where the family and their guests sat at the high table, and the rest of the household sat below or served, was a remnant of feudal England still not banished from the realm of the Tudors. Ceremony, particularly the ceremony of the salt, with its emphasis on due placing above or below it, still played a part in the life of the nobility. The architectural styles of the Renaissance abroad, though seldom practised by English architects, were readily copied by the silversmiths for the monumental salts, standing cups, ewers and other ceremonial plate of the sixteenth century. Renaissance motifs, with their chased foliage and flowers, swags of fruit and warrior figure finials, were also echoed in the hangings and embroideries, the carved decoration of the otherwise heavy and often ungainly furniture. Such pomp and panoply, like the processions and pageants and the rich clothes and colourful liveries, were no doubt palliatives for the harshness of life in the sixteenth century.

The rarity of Tudor silver makes every piece of special interest. Not all Tudor silver was of good quality, either of workmanship or strength of metal. But most pieces, other than spoons, are unique – perhaps the only, albeit exceptional, examples of their kind in any particular year; a single piece of silver may be the sole survivor of all that one maker produced; the mark or symbol can seldom be identified, and preservation of the piece was more often than not a matter of luck. It now stands alone as a relic of an age of opulence "wherein gold and silver most aboundeth".

PLATE 1

Mounted bowls, cups and jugs were popular from early mediaeval times. Wood—especially the spotted maple—pottery, ostrich eggs, mother-of-pearl and rock crystal, serpentine and rare porcelain from the east were all made into useful or ornamental vessels by the addition of silver or other mounts. Relatively large numbers of mediaeval mazer bowls survive, the band around the lip often carrying inscriptions, and the base with a medallion or "print", perhaps engraved with a religious emblem. This mazer of fifteenth-century date is $4\frac{3}{4}$ in. in diameter and has a later foot of about 1620.

PLATE 2

This typical example of tigerware, mounted in silver, of 1577, 10 in. high, bears the London hallmarks and the maker's mark, WC, a grasshopper below—probably for ▼ William Cocknidge.

PLATE 3

Of unexpected simplicity in Gothic England is the Cressener Cup of 1503, made in the year that work began on the fan-vaulted glory of Henry VII's Chapel in Westminster Abbey. The font-shaped bowl stands on a plain trumpet foot, the cover terminates in a flat enamelled print bearing the owner's arms (above). The cup is only $6\frac{3}{8}$ in. high. Since it was made in 1503 by a silversmith using a cross-bow as his mark, the cup has scarcely changed hands. It was in the possession of the Cressener family until 1722, and of the Tufnells from then until 1908 when it was purchased by the Gold-smiths' Company.

▶

PLATE 4

At the mediaeval and Tudor high table, there was much significance attached to the Great Salt, and where guests were placed in relation to it. Salt was a substance of ceremony, and silversmiths lavished great care on producing extravagant plate to hold the precious mineral. Rock crystal, enclosing gilded figures, elaborate architectural styles and as much skilful decoration as possible were almost obligatory for the great salts of the Elizabethan period, though few were made after the turn of the century. A rare latecomer was the Butleigh Salt of 1606, now in the Barber Institute of Fine Art at Birmingham. In the form of a tetrastyle shrine, four Corinthian columns enclose a scale-decorated central column which supports the small salt bowl hidden below the domed cover.

PLATE 5

Elizabethan ornament, always derived from Renaissance designs, could be crustily embossed and chased or extremely simple, a series perhaps of engraved lines or "hit-and-miss" hyphen-like ornament as seen on many Communion cups of the period. The Hutton Cup, made in 1589, has its spreading bowl and domed cover boldly engraved with formal sprays of scrolling foliage and flowerheads in most orderly array. By tradition the cup was a present from Queen Elizabeth I to her god-daughter Elizabeth Bowes, probably for her wedding in 1592, though an inscription on the cup, of later date, states that the gift was made in 1570.

PLATE 6

Less ostentatious than the architectural great salt of tradition was the late Elizabethan bell salt which came into fashion about 1590. Arranged in three sections, the lower and middle parts bell out below the domed upper part which contains a small perforated section screwed into the top. The two lower sections contain shallow depressions for salt, and the whole salt stands on three ball feet. Most of these salts were decorated with chased scrolls and strapwork on a matted ground—as the one illustrated here, though simpler engraved bell salts are also recorded. The salt shown is $8\frac{3}{4}$ in. high, weighs 10 oz. 7 dwt., and was made in 1599; the maker's mark is apparently a bell which appears between initials.

PLATE 7

The beaker with its tapering sides and slightly everted lip was, until the coming of glass at the end of the seventeenth century, one of the most universal of all drinking vessels. Large silver beakers, between $5\frac{1}{2}$ and $6\frac{1}{2}$ in. high, were usual in the James I period, and here was an almost uniform pattern of engraved arabesques and strapwork with pendant motifs around the top, and stamped ovolos and similar formal decoration round the spreading rim foot. This beaker with its stylised scroll, thistle and strapwork ornament is $5\frac{3}{4}$ in. high, weighs 9 oz. 17 dwt. It is engraved "Mychaell Hampe 1608", for the Mitchell family of Hamp, Somerset. It was in fact made in 1608, by a maker using the mark GC, with a mullet above and below. ▶

1600–1660

"Into pikes and musqueteers
"Stampt beakers, cups and porringers."

The dissolution of the monasteries, the exigencies of war and taxation, the vagaries of fashion and the ravages of time all took heavy toll of early English silver. The sixty years from 1600 to 1660 forced most of what had survived those depredations into the melting-pot, or sent them overseas – like the vast presents sent by a wildly generous James I to Castile on conclusion of the peace with Spain.

So little has survived from the pre-Restoration period that it is difficult to see how silversmithing developed before the melting-pots took over. The early years of the seventeenth century saw the introduction of the steeple cup, a peculiarly English form of standing cup with a steeple-like finial to the cover. One hundred and forty-nine are known to exist, which gives an indication of how many must in fact have been made.

Before his urgent need for plate for money, Charles I was no mean patron of the silversmith. He favoured Dutch styles, particularly the lobed and flowing mode of Van Vianen. Dutch flower and foliate designs soon began to supersede the older Renaissance motifs, only to be cut short by the Civil War. Though the king was dead and an uneasy peace reigned, the Commonwealth years were lean times for the silversmith. Silver was in short supply, luxuries of all kinds were frowned upon by the Puritan-led government, and most patrons were either impoverished or exiled. Many silversmiths must have closed up their workshops altogether, and for a decade (with some notable exceptions) only a few, usually lightweight and poorly decorated silverwares were made. No doubt the silversmiths were chief among those "in a merry mood because of the king's coming" when 1660 dawned.

PLATE 8

This tankard is a survival of Elizabethan renaissance style. The thumbpiece is in the form of a winged female figure. The handle is a plain bold scroll, the cover is flat and peaked, and carries the maker's mark, RP, the London hallmarks and date letter for 1638.

PLATE 9

Until the beginning of the eighteenth century silver goblets were still made in fairly large quantities, sometimes decorated with engraving or repoussé chasing sometimes plain except for perhaps an engraved coat-of-arms in a plumed cartouche. On this wine cup, $5\frac{3}{4}$ in. high, the arms are in a crossed laurel wreath. The cup, which weighs 4 oz. 10 dwt., was made in 1639. The maker's mark appears to be a bird with an olive branch above initials, one of which is T.

PLATE 10

There is in the Ashmolean Museum at Oxford an unmarked, silver-mounted box, its lid formed of an actual scallop shell. Several of these small boxes of silver, usually termed spice or sugar caskets, were made during the early years of the seventeenth century; the earliest and richest in fact dates from 1598 and is in the collection of the Middle Temple in London, its sides beautifully chased with scrolls, flowerheads and strapwork of a high order. The top is typically chased to represent a scallop shell and the four feet are also formed as shells. More usually, as on this box of 1612, the sides were plain and the feet were either shells, or, as here, snails. This box is $5\frac{1}{2}$ in. long and weighs 12 oz. 2 dwt.

PLATE 11

In a country where most silver went into the melting-pot to pay
the taxes levied by Charles I, it is strange that a fairly large number
of shallow saucer-dishes should have survived from the 1630's.
Most were quite small—about 5 in. across. More than half these
little saucer-dishes made between 1630 and 1640 appear to have been
the work of William Maundy, and his business was apparently
continued by Thomas Maundy—two of the few silversmiths of the
periods whose marks have been identified. This saucer was made by
William Maundy in 1634, is $5\frac{1}{2}$ in. in diameter, but weighs only
3 oz. 5 dwt.—indicative of the shortage of silver at the period.

PLATE 12

One of the few really outstanding silversmiths during the Charles I
and Commonwealth periods was a maker using a hound sejant as his
mark. His work is unexceptionally fine, and these two flagons from
Thirkleby, Yorkshire, are superb examples of mid-seventeenth
century chasing in the best Dutch style. Each flagon is 10 in. high and
has panels of dolphins and sea-monsters amid scrolling foliage and
flowers. The panel on the front is engraved with the arms of Tyssen,
a family of Dutch-born merchants. Made in 1646, the flagons weigh
73 oz.

1660-1700

"19th October, 1664. Weighed my two silver flaggons at Stevens's. They weigh 212 oz. 27 dwt. which is about £50 at 5s. per oz.: and then they judge the fashion to be worth about 5s. per oz. more; nay, some say 10s. an ounce the fashion. Sorry to see that the fashion is worth so much, and the silver come to no more . . .

"February 2nd, 1665. With my wife looked over our plate, and picked out £40 worth, I believe, to change for more useful plate, to our great content, and then we shall have a very handsome cupboard of plate."

Samuel Pepys: Diary

It was half show, half desire for silver for the home and the table, that dictated the prosperity of the silversmiths after the Restoration. The poor were very poor, but there was a growing population of tradesmen, skilled craftsmen and minor gentry with fast-increasing incomes. Life in the home was daily becoming more comfortable – the first upholstered wing armchairs came in during the reign of Charles II: there were day beds and couches, tapestries decorated the walls, rich cloths covered the table-tops, carpets were soon to find their place on the floor. To acquire a cupboardful of plate to serve food and drink, not forgetting the three rapidly accepted beverages – tea, coffee and chocolate – was the aim of every man who prided himself on a good house.

The seventeenth century was an era of great experiment and scientific investigation. Aesthetically, the forty years from the Restoration to 1700 saw almost as many variant styles in silver as there were years. Dutch influence predominated, retrospectively at first, though by the end of the century it had been given a new stimulus by the arrival of Dutch William on the throne. Between-times, there were fashions for chinoiserie and for the French *Régence* styles that, with the arrival of hundreds of refugee Huguenots from France, were soon to overtake the Dutch styles and bring silversmithing in England to its finest period.

PLATE 13

The ceremony and splendour of
the Elizabethan high table was
largely forgotten after the Restoration, but occasionally memories
of it lingered on in later plate,
especially that made for the City
Livery Companies. One such piece
was the silver-gilt standing salt
made about 1662, when it was
seen and noted by Samuel Pepys
the diarist. The salt is an elabora-
tion of the octagonal spool form,
with a rock crystal body. The base
rests on eight small lions couchant, while cherubs' heads and
wings displayed decorate the
sides; four eagles with wings
displayed and four small hounds
are set on orbs round the top.
It was made to the order of Ports-
mouth Corporation for presentation to Queen Catherine of Bra-
ganza on her marriage to Charles
II. When the Queen returned to
Portugal in 1692, she apparently
sold the salt to Thomas Seymour,
who had it inscribed and presented it to the Goldsmiths' Company.

PLATE 14

Tankards were made in silver holding as much as three or four pints, and one massive example of 1690 is recorded as holding no less than six pints. Average tankards, however, are usually about 6 in. high. The Charles II type, with its plain body, usually only relieved by an engraved coat-of-arms, its flat cap cover with a peaked front, its bifurcated scroll or corkscrew thumbpiece, scroll handle and plain rim foot set the style until the eighteenth century. This example of 1661, by a maker marking with an Orb and Cross, weighs 25 oz. and stands 6 in. high. Note the typical placing of the hallmarks.

PLATE 15

Porringers and covers, often with bulging bodies embossed with bold
naturalistic chasing, are typical of the domestic silver of the Restoration period. The Janus-like finials often show tragic and comic
masks, while lion and unicorn motifs were also popular. This cup,
formerly in the possession of the Coldstream Guards, is repoussé
chased with a lion on one side, a goat on the other, amid flowers and
foliage. It is $7\frac{1}{2}$ in. high, weighs 29 oz. 10 dwt., and was made in 1663.
The cover, by the same maker, H.G., dates from 1661.

PLATE 17 ▶

Silver for display was usually influenced by the richly overall-chased Dutch designs. Even firedogs and furniture were made of silver, while garnitures for the mantelpiece, in the style of pottery jars and vases, were another silver luxury. Ovoid jars with domed covers, usually known as ginger jars, were the most usual form for this decorative silver. This jar, from a pair made about 1675 (maker's mark, IB, with a crescent below) is 10½ in. high and is richly and finely embossed and chased with an amorino on either side playing a trumpet in a forest of scrolling foliage on a matted ground. Others, usually a little larger, were embossed and chased with alternating lobes and leaf strapwork, and might be festooned with fruit and floral garlands around the domed, bud-finialled cover.

PLATE 16

The candlesticks of the Charles II period were generally columnar, with square or hexagonal bases, and broad drip pans at the tops. As the century wore on, drip pans became smaller and the columns were fluted. Sometimes the bases were enriched with acanthus leaf or other embossed chasing. In size, candlesticks were from about 8 in. to as much as 12 in. high, and sets of two or four were not uncommon. The pair shown belongs to Hereford Corporation, and was made in 1666 by one of the most prolific and best London makers of the period, who used a mark of a crowned S, often ascribed to Charles Shelley. The sconces are by another maker and date from 1670. ▼

In the years of silver shortage, cut-card decoration served the purpose of strengthening handle and foot joints as well as being ornamental, but it was also much used on relatively heavy pieces of silver—as on this beautiful oval casket with cut-card decoration above the cast feet and round the looped-snake handle. The box, which is 8 in. long and weighs 20 oz. 15 dwt., was perhaps for sugar.

PLATE 20

This large tankard of 1677, 7¾ in. high, follows the typical seventeenth century style, though the silversmith (known only by his mark, IA, in a beaded oval) has been influenced by the continental baroque style with its emphasis on cast chased ornament.

◀ PLATE 19

The Act enforcing higher standard silver in 1696 did much to regularise the marking of silver. Most of the unmarked, or maker's mark only, silver antedates the Act. This fine, heavy cup and cover, in the almost straight-sided baroque style that succeeded the rather florid ogee-shaped bowls of early Charles II porringers, has the maker's mark, HW, in a shaped punch, on both body and cover. It is heavy, weighing 28 oz. 2 dwt., and is 6 in. in height. On style it can be dated to c. 1680.

PLATE 21

The reeded border, the pierced back
handle with its beaded rib and its engraved
coat-of-arms in a plumed cartouche all
corroborate the evidence of the hallmarks
which show that this snuffer tray was made
by Francis Garthorne, a leading London
goldsmith, in 1678. The tray is accompanied
by a pair of undated contemporary snuffers
by another maker. It is rare to find tray
and snuffers by the same maker. The
snuffers were scissor-like implements, with
a box at the axis, used for wick-trimming.

PLATE 22

The earliest example of sheathing a plain
silver-gilt lining with a casing of pierced
and chased silver is dated 1669. This rare
and interesting style was followed even
as late as about 1685, however, when a
silversmith, probably Thomas Issod, made
this cup and cover, from the collection of
the Goldsmiths' Company. The inner drum
is silver-gilt, and the outer sleeve silver-
pierced and chased with foliage and birds
in the Dutch manner, with a peacock on
one side and a turkey on the other.

▲ PLATE 24

Since toilet sets were fashionable, it is not surprising that the fashion for chinoiseries should have affected them, and brushes, caskets, boxes and bottles were often engraved or flat chased with charmingly naïve dreams of the land from which tea, spices and porcelain were now arriving in increasing quantities. This octagonal casket from a toilet set of 1683, shows typical birds, flowers and hunters.

PLATE 23

Most functional mugs and cups were plain—even without arms, suggesting that they were the silver of the middle classes rather than the gentry, and initials or at best a monogram were the usual key to ownership. These two small mugs have the typical hand-raised bulbous body on a rim foot, reeded neck and fluted scroll handle. The larger, 4 in. high, was made in 1688, the smaller, $3\frac{1}{2}$ in. high, dates from 1683.

▶

PLATE 25

Beakers followed forms as traditional as mugs, and were made in all sizes and also as barrel-like pairs—double beakers. Beakers of tapered cylindrical form on a moulded foot were made throughout the length and breadth of the country and even survived the arrival of glasses and better pottery. Usually about 3 or 4 in. high, decorated styles followed the current fashion for engraving, chinoiserie flat chasing, acanthus embossing and the like—as this small beaker of 1688 with its figure of a strutting Chinaman among sketchily worked trees, plants and birds. The plain beaker was made ten years later, in 1698, by George Garthorne, who by then had to use the higher Britannia standard silver for his work.

PLATE 26

The arrival of the Huguenot craftsmen in England brought many changes to English styles and techniques. A refinement of ornament was one of the most striking contributions of the Huguenots even when they were making wares in typically English form. Here Pierre Harache, the first of the refugee silversmiths to be admitted to the Freedom of the Goldsmiths' Company, gives the piercing of the caster top a delicacy and detail missing in the work of most English silversmiths. His treatment of the base and the bottom of the cover, with its formal gadrooned border, reflects the ordered style of the Huguenots, while even the treatment of the coat-of-arms is more elaborate. This caster was made in 1690.

PLATE 27

Development of the sugar plantations in the West Indies during the seventeenth century meant that sugar, though still expensive, was much more plentiful in late Stuart England than it had been at the beginning of the century. Large cylindrical casters were made during the second half of the seventeenth century, often appearing in sets of three, one large caster for sugar, and a pair of smaller ones for pepper and dry mustard. Keeping the pierced top in place when inverting the caster resulted in the rather clumsy bayonet joint. Piercing was usually rather coarse, and the moulded rim foot was frequently also pierced out en suite with the top. This straight-sided caster, made in 1690, bears the maker's mark BB.

PLATE 28

Gadrooning and fluting were the principal keynotes of the later Dutch baroque, a style wholeheartedly accepted by the London silversmiths. A seventeenth-century newcomer to the silversmith's range had been the salver, often made to match tankards or porringers to save "the Carpit (i.e. tablecloth) or Cloathes from drops". The uses for salvers were, in fact, legion, and they remained a stable line for the silversmith throughout the eighteenth century. Early salvers were often provided with a detachable trumpet foot. This salver, by Robert Cooper, 1691, has foot and border gadrooned.

PLATE 29

Some silversmiths still clung to older styles, even in 1691. This small two-handled porringer, engraved with chinoiseries, features the rather slender scroll handles that superseded the even spindlier caryatid handles. By now, however, most porringers, with or without covers, were coming to be decorated with half-fluting around the lower part of the body, the upper part being slightly everted and girdled with a band of cording. Between the fluting and the rib an embossed and chased baroque cartouche for crest or initials was often provided.

E.S.   K

PLATE 30 ▲

The earliest known baluster candlesticks were the work of Pierre
Harache in 1683, soon after his admission by the London goldsmiths,
but within two or three years leading London makers had followed
suit with baluster sticks, on moulded octagonal bases with slightly
sunk centres, knopped stems and cylindrical sockets. Baluster
candlesticks of this type, usually between 5 in. and 7 in. high were
made in pairs, fours, and sixes with little variation until about 1718.
The pair shown above were made by Ralph Leeke in 1690.

PLATE 31 ▶

The gadrooned candlesticks (right), dated 1699, are a late example
of the baroque style by Pierre Harache, though gadrooning had more
or less gone out of fashion altogether by about 1705. A variation
of the gadrooned baluster stick was that with small applied lion
masks at the shoulders. From the same period date a number of
figure candlesticks, with fluted sockets upheld by kneeling blacka-
moors or draped female figures and even survival of the straight
columnar type with fluted and reeded stem and octagonal base.

PLATE 33

A rare instance of Scandinavian influence on English silver at a time when Scandinavian silversmiths were themselves beginning to copy English tea and coffee silver is this large tankard of 1692 by Robert Cooper. As well as the lion couchant feet and thumbpiece, the tankard shows Scandinavian influence in the broad reeded bands at and a little above the base, and in the slightly domed cover. The front of the body carries a coat-of-arms of rather later date.

▶

PLATE 32

Isaac Dighton, a maker who seems to have favoured the panels enclosed by spiral scrolls on more than one punch bowl, made this one in 1699. It is 11 in. in diameter, weighs 55 oz. 18 dwt. and is now at Temple Newsam House, Leeds. ▼

PLATE 34 ▲

Benjamin Pyne, a prominent and prolific London silversmith, while
objecting to Huguenots opening workshops in London, employed a
French design for the beautifully flat chased and engraved ornament
of his octagonal dishes of 1698—and probably a French craftsman to
do the work as well. The dishes, with a border of cupids, animals
and foliage, have a most elaborately engraved coat-of-arms contained
in a scrolling, foliate and cupid-surmounted cartouche.

PLATE 35   While the Huguenots were slowly establishing themselves and their
baluster styles, the English silversmiths continued to work in the
baroque manner, though even they followed the French lead towards
taller cups and covers. A scalloped matted band and punched motifs,
however, betrayed the English makers, and while both English and
Huguenot silversmiths used gadrooning extensively, beaded handles
seem to have been a native motif. This cup and cover $11\frac{1}{4}$in. high and
weighing 46 oz. 8 dwt., was made in 1699 by John Sutton. ▶

PLATE 36

Even as late as 1763 when Tobias Smollett went on his travels to France and Italy, he took with him the necessaries of gentlemanly living—linen, books and, not least, a modicum of silverwares. On all outdoor occasions, the travelling set was a useful pocket companion, and the most comprehensive included a beaker or tumbler-cup, knife, fork and spoon with detachable handles, double spice box for salt and pepper, nutmeg grater in its cylindrical case, apple corer, toothpick, and corkscrew. Spoons and forks of such sets were usually by specialist makers, and it is not unusual to find most of the pieces unmarked or only partly marked. In this set, which folds neatly into a green velvet covered block inside the tumbler, the cup is by Charles Overing, 1701, and is delightfully and typically engraved with a hunting scene. The three hooks may have been for napkins.

PLATE 37

Baroque styles lingered on into the Queen Anne period. This punch bowl—often called a Monteith from its scalloped rim—shows a refining of the late baroque style, with its straight-fluted sides. For the rest, however, the decoration is typical of the later seventeenth century, with the moulded and gadrooned, circular foot, the scrolling leaf and scale cartouche, the scalloped border echoing the fluting of the body, and the stylised cherub head, scroll and strapwork rim. Weighing exactly 69 oz., the bowl measures $10\frac{3}{4}$ in. in diameter, and was made by Richard Syng in 1705.

PLATE 38

Salt, no longer the condiment of ceremony, still had its place at table, and the small trencher salt, often cast, was a pleasing feature of the dinner service. The taller, spool-shaped individual salts of the later seventeenth century were replaced by small, low ones, sometimes plain, sometimes decorated as here. A favourite style was the octagonal, with stepped moulded sides. These four circular salts, on gadrooned, moulded bases, have boldly fluted sides and circular wells. They were made by Edmund Proctor in 1701.

"Coffee, tea and chocolate are now become capital branches of this nation's commerce."

Daniel Defoe: *The Review*, 1713

While Queen Anne's generals and admirals fought abroad, trade and manufacture were rapidly developing at home. New discoveries and undertakings, new customs and an unabated taste for the luxuries of life all stimulated craftsmanship. London, the only really large city in the whole country, won a special place not only as a centre of trade and business, but for its glittering, gambling, social life as well. "Trade is the wealth of the world," cried Defoe, yet he saw with some dismay how even the pastry-cooks set out their wares on silver salvers. And this was in a period when only the higher and more expensive Britannia-standard silver was used.

The fashionable world, which included the literary and the political, not only collected fine things for themselves, but delighted in going to see the wealth of others, visiting the palaces and villas, the grand colonnaded terraces and landscaped parklands, created for the nobility by Hawksmoor, Vanbrugh and Gibbs. Inside their houses, elegance was the keynote: fine walnut furniture, gilded and upholstered chairs and settees, silken hangings, pretty side tables and writing desks, mirrors, chandeliers and wall sconces. The taste for pictures and porcelain, glass and plate kept the craftsmen busy for all sections of society – and especially the silversmith, greatly assisted by the needs of the tea-table in the salon and the capacities of the men's drinking parties in the dining-room.

PLATE 39 ▶

Even without the mark of Pierre Platel, the silversmith who taught Paul De Lamerie his craft, this cup and cover is unmistakably of Huguenot origin. The applied strapwork, with its husks and guilloche ornament within spoon-like surrounds, the formal leaf cut-card on the cover with its fine finial, the harp handles and the somewhat elongated body all suggest Huguenot work. Note also the exceptionally fine engraved coat-of-arms. The cup was made in 1702.

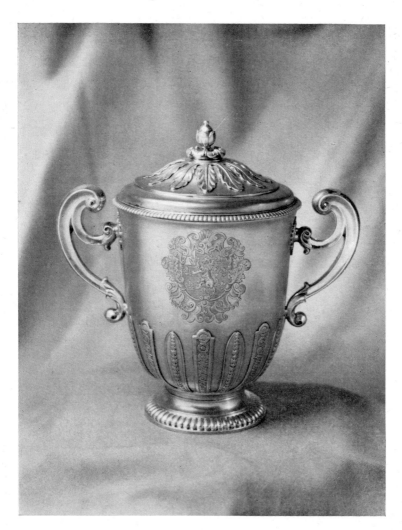

PLATE 40

Soon the silversmiths mastered the style that was to dominate coffee and chocolate-pot design for the next two decades. They retained the slightly tapered, cylindrical body, often even the scrolling cut-card work, of the seventeenth century. But they gave the pots a new grace and dignity with a curved spout, sometimes provided with a hinged cap, and by using a high-domed cover topped with a baluster finial. The handle was set at right angles to the spout, the continental practice of using a straight, horizontal side handle not generally finding favour in England. This coffee-pot of 1701, just under 10 in. high and weighing 25 oz. 12 dwt., was made in London by Anthony Nelme. The leather-covered handle is decorated with a silver strap, and the high-domed cover with acorn finial is fluted and matted in the English baroque manner.

PLATE 41

Tea, coffee and chocolate, all introduced to England about 1650, had more impact on silverwares than any other drink. At first the silversmiths were undecided how best to shape the pots for the new beverages. For coffee and chocolate they adapted the cylindrical form of the tankard and flagon, tapering the body, and adding a straight spout and a conical cover. Indeed, one of the first teapots known also followed this form, although a pattern based on the Chinese wine-pot with a curved spout really set the style for teapots. In this conical coffee-pot by Andrew Raven, made in 1700, cut-card work gives decorative detail at the junction of the sockets for the D-shaped handle which is at right angles to the rather unimposing straight spout.

PLATE 42

Of all the silver forms introduced by the Huguenots, the helmet-shaped ewer was most typical. This superb example by Pierre Harache was made in 1703, and illustrates his mastery of modelling, of applied strapwork and use of a decorative mask in association with moulding

and gadrooning. The figure handle was a favourite with Harache, as was the mask of Diana—on a shell below the shaped, moulded lip. The ewer is 12 in. high, and weighs 69 oz. 11 dwt. It bears the arms of Methuen engraved in a most elaborate baroque cartouche.

PLATE 44

The baluster form was early
adopted for the sugar caster
especially by silversmiths of
Huguenot origin, who also favoured applied or flat chased ornament
and designed intricate, pierced
patterns for the tops. This large
caster, 8¼ in. high, is from a pair by
Lewis Mettayer. The outward-
curved baluster form is eight-
panelled and chased with strapwork on a matted ground. An
unusual feature is the method of
securing the scroll-pierced cover,
a slip-lock being used to obviate
the usual clumsy bayonet clamps.
The casters, made in 1705, are
each engraved on the bases with
their original weights—20 = 4
and 22 = 17—instancing the heavy
silver of the period.

◀

Trios of casters continued to be made throughout the eighteenth century, often by specialist makers. From the early years of the century, the pear shape ousted the old straight-sided type. The bodies were often encircled by a moulded rib, flanged bayonet joints secured the covers, now usually pierced in flower and scroll patterns. This set, the tallest $7\frac{1}{2}$ in. high, the pair 6 in. high, weighs 19 oz. 17 dwt., and was made by John Jackson in 1709.

PLATE 45   ▲

Early teapots were usually small, probably due to the extremely high cost of tea. This pear-shaped teapot, quite plain except for a coat-of-arms in a baroque cartouche engraved on the side, has a faceted swan-neck spout with hinged cover, very high-domed cover and turned wood-scroll handle. It was made by Benjamin Pyne in 1707. Of the same date is the tripod stand on scroll and bun feet supporting a circular lamp, and with wood side handle. The stand was made by Isaac Liger. The pot and the stand are $8\frac{1}{2}$ in. high overall.

PLATE 47 ▶

Chocolate-pot and coffee-pot designs are often indistinguishable, except for the aperture in the cover through which the stirring rod for the chocolate can be inserted. In the early years of the eighteenth century, a tall, tapered cylinder, with wood scroll handle and curved spout at right angles to the handle, was the usual form. This chocolate-pot by Gabriel Sleath, made in 1709, has plain flange-like cards encircling the spout and handle sockets. The high-domed cover has hinged flap below the baluster finial, and a simple thumbpiece with double-corkscrew terminals.

PLATE 46

With small teapots, large kettles were needed to ensure plenty of hot water for replenishment. This tea-kettle and stand, made by Lewis Mettayer in 1708, is of exceptionally large size. It stands $16\frac{1}{2}$ in. high and weighs no less than 128 oz. The design is typical of the Queen Anne and George I periods, with circular pear-shaped body, faceted swan-neck spout with so-called duck's head terminal, domed cover and swing handle. Sometimes the body was octagonal. The tripod scroll stand and lamp have heavy cast supports and a circular grooved well for the base of the kettle.

◀

PLATE 48

Not all Queen Anne silver was in the simple style that has come to be called after her. Indeed, it was often very elaborate, especially that made for royalty and for the nobility. One of a pair, this pilaster sconce, 19¾ in. high, weighing 76 oz. 10 dwt., was made by David Willaume in 1707. The arms of the owner, James Boyle, Duke of Queensbury and his wife, form an integral part of the design, chased in relief above the foliate grotesque mask from which springs the candle branch. Above the achievement, a circular Garter medallion, crest and ducal coronet form the top of wall plate of each of the sconces.

PLATE 49

By the second decade of the eighteenth century, few pieces were made in wholly Huguenot or wholly English style. This magnificent cup and cover by Anthony Nelme (1715), is boldly modelled, with sturdy applied work round the base of the bell-shaped bowl, which is girdled by a heavy moulded rib; above this is engraved a fine and elaborate coat-of-arms. The harp-shaped handles are ornamented with applied scrollwork and with formal flowerheads, while the circular foot and domed cover are chased with gadroons and scrolls.

▶

PLATE 50 ▲

Everything that could be fashioned
in silver had its admirers, and
small trays for inkpots, snuffers
and even spoons for the teatable
were made in large numbers. This
oval snuffer tray has a raised
moulded rim, and relies for its
decoration on the scrollwork
back-handle and the engraved
coat-of-arms at the centre. It
stands on four ball feet and is
8¼ in. long. It was made by John
Chartier in 1712.

▲
PLATE 51 One of the most charming styles of dish at this period was the type
with fluted sides and scalloped rim, usually termed a strawberry
dish—though probably used for all kinds of desserts. This dish
made in 1719 by Richard Bayley, is just under 7 in. in diameter,
weighs 9 oz. 7 dwt. Note how the armorials inscribed after assay
have been engraved off-centre to avoid the hallmarks.

▲ PLATE 52

Here the unusual seven-sided form is used for the curved spout of an octagonal coffee-pot, on moulded base and with octagonal domed cover. $9\frac{1}{2}$ in. high, and weighing 24 oz. 5 dwt., this pot by Richard Bayley, dated 1718, is typical in size and weight of coffee-pots of the period, and shows haphazard placing of hallmarks.

PLATE 53

Even without the elegant cartouches surrounding the engraved
coats-of-arms, this trio of casters
shows the slight trend towards
decoration making its appearance
in the 1720's. The slide-in octagonal tops of these casters have the
pierced vases of flowers and formal
scroll and leaf designs accentuated
by engraving, though simplicity is
still the keynote of the moulded
girdles, stepped bases and acorn
finials. The tall caster stands 8 in.
high, the pair 6½ in. They were
made by Edmund Pearce in 1720.

▼

PLATE 55

Usually of heavy gauge silver,
sauce-boats after about 1712 were
given interest by means of shaped,
moulded rims and scroll handles
on either side. This pair, on oval
moulded feet, shows the armorials
of the owner placed on one side.
They are 8½ in. long, weigh
together 27 oz. 15 dwt., and were
made in 1721 by Sarah Holaday.
Her mark, in a widow's lozenge,
was registered in 1719, but like
most women silversmiths, she
probably supervised the workshop
and did not make silver herself.

▶

PLATE 54 ▶

Small, covered jugs, probably used for warm milk or cream, presaged the baluster form later to be taken by coffee- and chocolate-pots and jugs. Though tea was originally taken plain, by the 1720's both sugar and warmed cream became fashionable at the tea-table, and this small covered jug with its raised moulded foot to keep the heat of the contents well away from the tabletop was both functional and attractive. Made by William Fawdery in 1719, it is $5\frac{1}{2}$ in. and weighs 7 oz.

PLATE 56

Candlesticks and candelabra of the first forty years of the eighteenth century retained the baluster form. Here the hexagonal form is chosen for the moulded bases and tapered stems of a pair of table candlesticks by Thomas Mason, dated 1725. Each is 7 in. high, and they weigh together 25 oz. 5 dwt. The sunk circular wells are engraved, quite typically for the period, with armorials, and the hexagonal form is followed through to the moulded sconces.

PLATE 57

A more decorative variation was the candlestick with rather cushion-like, shaped and moulded base, though here the octagonal still shows its influence, both on the base and the tapered stem. This style was the immediate predecessor of the early rococo candlestick, with the panels on the stem and foot providing a ground for chased strapwork and other ornament. This attractive pair of candlesticks, weighing together 23 oz. 5 dwt., was made by Matthew Cooper in 1727.

PLATE 58

The Walpole Salver by Paul De Lamerie was made in 1728 to commemorate Sir Robert Walpole's holding of the Exchequer Seal of George I. 19¼ in. square, the salver weighs 135 oz. 7 dwt. The guilloche border is mounted on an upcurved rim chased with trelliswork; the inner border is chased and engraved with strapwork and foliage. The engraved central medallion is possibly by Hogarth.

PLATE 59

A superb example of silversmithing and a reflection of the mannered *Régence* style of decoration supremely handled by a young silversmith is this silver charger, made in 1722 by Lamerie. It is engraved in what is known as the Hogarthian style and, indeed, may even be the work of Hogarth, though he soon left the craft he had trained for. The charger is 21½ in. in diameter.

▲ PLATE 60

These salts could have been made in any year from 1700 to 1725. Each engraved with a coat-of-arms, they are typical examples of the cast, octagonal trencher salts of the period, usually made in sets of two, four or more. These, dated 1720, are by John White.

PLATE 61

A typical sugar bowl with cover, made by William Fordham in 1730.

◀

PLATE 62 ▲

Tea-table silver of the 1720's was frequently quite plain, relying for its attraction on the beauty of its moulded line and the engraver's skill at conceiving a fine cartouche about the owner's coat-of-arms. The tea-table hostess frequently blended her own teas at the table, so that more than one caddy was essential. The tea canister, with sliding base and bottle top, was popular. This pair, made in 1726, have moulded octagonal bodies, their simplicity relieved only by the engraved coats-of-arms in baroque cartouches on each front.

PLATE 63 ▶

A touch of the grotesque for the lion masks at the knuckles of a circular salt on four paw feet; it is from a set of four made by Paul De Lamerie in 1731. Similar salts, with lion mask and paw decoration, became popular throughout the whole of the rococo period.

PLATE 65 ▶

This fine, small ewer is only $8\frac{3}{4}$ in. high, yet incorporates all the features of the larger rosewater ewers still made for ceremony. The moulded rib below the double-scroll handle, with its outstanding female bust terminal, shows the superb feeling of the craftsman for movement as it swells out into scrolls around engraved arms below the lip, itself in scrolling foliate form that is echoed in the engraved strap-work, foliage, masks and shells below the shaped rim. Below, simple applied "spoon-handle" straps contrast with the incipient rococoism of the upper part. It was made by Crespin in 1727.

PLATE 64

Made in the same year as the Walpole salver, this fine two-handled cup and cover is also by Paul De Lamerie, and shows the growing trend towards more decorative silver. The cup, with its scroll handles and moulded rib encircling the body, is of a style made by Lamerie and others at the period. Indeed one cup (of 1726) by Lamerie is almost identical with this one except for its plainness. Here, however, Lamerie adds intricate applied detail to the base of the bowl and to the domed cover, and enriches the upper part with borders of trelliswork and foliage around fine coats-of-arms in baroque cartouches, engraved on either side. The cup, made in 1728 and weighing 61 oz. 3 dwt., stands $10\frac{5}{8}$ in. high.

▲ PLATE 66

A fine simple punch bowl on circular moulded foot, engraved with a
coat-of-arms within a circular medallion. It is $9\frac{1}{4}$ in. in diameter,
weighs 33 oz. 8 dwt., and was made by Thomas Farrer in 1731. Bowls
of this type were in fact made from the early years of the century,
and continued in fashion until about 1770, early examples usually
having a detachable rim which was often scalloped.

PLATE 67

In complete contrast with the simplicity of silver for beer and punch, this cup and cover by Paul De Lamerie, 1733, shows the swirling themes of the rococo overlaid on the simple form of two-handled cup and cover. At the base of the bowl, twisted leaf shapes are applied on a matted ground, with scrolling foliage and scalework from a border between the rim and the central moulded rib, enclosing an elaborate coat-of-arms in a baroque cartouche. More leafage swirls around the scroll handles and up the domed cover to the finial. This confection in silver, only 12½ in. high, weighs 72 oz. 3 dwt. ▼

PLATE 68

Baskets for cake, bread and fruit were known from Tudor times, and in this pair of 1734 Paul De Lamerie harked back to a much earlier style. By the early years of the eighteenth century, most baskets were oval, and the swing handle design rapidly became popular, though some baskets continued to be made with end handles. Until the mid 1730's, piercing was usually formal and repetitive, many baskets simulating wickerwork. Only $5\frac{1}{2}$ in. high, these two baskets weigh together 81 oz. 10 dwt.

PLATE 69

A salver and tray maker of considerable reputation in the middle years of the eighteenth century was John Tuite, whose virtuosity is elegantly portrayed here in a large, oblong tea-tray. A broad band of strapwork enclosing husks, shells, scrolls, foliage and flowerheads is intersected by classical masks, and follows the shaped, moulded rim of the tray. In the centre, en suite, is a coat-of-arms in a scrolling baroque cartouche. John Tuite made this tray in 1732. It weighs 115 oz., and is $22\frac{1}{2}$ in. long.

PLATE 70 ▲

Basically simple, of bullet shape on a rim foot, the teapot gradually
acquired some of the trappings of the rococo. Here, shells, scrolls
and strapwork overlap shoulders and flat lid, while the curved spout
is enriched with petal-like faceting and the upper handle-socket
is leaf-capped. The engraved arms, in foliate cartouche, repeat the
decorative theme of the rest of this piece. The pot, made by Gabriel
Sleath in 1733, weighs 13 oz. 2 dwt.

PLATE 71 ▶

Enrichment of the otherwise simple globular tea-kettle was made
easier by its having a stand and lamp. Here the faceted spout and
shoulders bear shell and scroll ornament, while the silversmith,
Edward Vincent, has been able to express the rococo love of decoration in the pierced apron concealing the lamp. Masks, fruit swags,
scrolls and foliage are pierced and chased between the paw-footed
tripod supports of the stand, of which even the frame at the top is
notched into a wavy-edge design. The kettle together with its stand
and lamp were all made by Vincent in 1734.

1735–1760

"Did I write you word that we had got a new terene? The chasing is mighty well done: it holds six quarts, and has a very light look."

Mrs. Delany: correspondence, 1745

Historically, there is little enough to differentiate the middle years of the eighteenth century from the reigns of Queen Anne and George I. Trade and manufacture continued to grow and prosper, London even faster, though a visitor in 1740 who had not seen London for thirty years or so would probably only note that it was yet more crowded, that gin and poverty were rampant, and that some elegant new houses had been built; it was rather in detail that there were changes – an inevitable transition to a more decorative manner. The Earl of Burlington and that "Apollo of the Arts . . . Mr. Kent" laid down the "Rules of Taste" to guide their patrons along Palladian lines. It was a new, lighter style of Palladianism, influenced by French and Italian originals – rich, sometimes gilded, usually relying on carved detail of shells, scrolls and grotesque masks. In silver this French fashion meant the curvaceous, much-chased and fantastic forms of the rococo; the simple baluster became the broken curve, neatly ordered, flat chased or engraved scrolls and strap-work were turned into chased scrolls, shells and rocky surfaces in high relief. And the same swirls and bombé curves underlie the mid-eighteenth century chinoiserie – "the barbarous gaudy gout of the Chinese" – which became the fashionable whim about 1740. English rococo had, perhaps, the saving grace of rather more restraint than French rococo, and it certainly showed good humour. By 1760, however, it had laughed itself out of favour.

PLATE 72

This very fine oval basket, made in 1736 by John White, has the sides pierced in a flowing design, picked out with engraving. The oval foot is also pierced out with scrollwork, while the everted rim is pierced into leaf designs and bordered with an unusual mount, formed of chased and matted guilloche pattern. The base and swing handle are engraved with yet more foliage and strapwork.

PLATE 74 Even in the great ages of decorative domestic silver, there was always a demand for less ornate styles, partly on account of taste, partly, no doubt, because of the expense of decoration. In the early rococo period, the tapered cylinder was still the predominating form for chocolate and coffee-pots, though by the 1730's the high-domed cover was distinctly out of date and most covers were much flatter. The rim foot, too, often spread out further. This fine choco-late-pot by Richard Beale, made in 1734, weighing 32 oz. 5 dwt. and $9\frac{1}{2}$ in. in height, is a good example of the plain style, its only con-cession to the new ornament being a beautiful cartouche swirling around the coat-of-arms on the side.

PLATE 73

One of the two Hardwicke tureens, made by Paul De Lamerie in 1734 and 1737, and now in The Minneapolis Museum of Art. They are of magnificent proportions, $13\frac{3}{4}$ in. long, and weighing together 359 oz. 13 dwt. The boldly modelled lion masks and the charming sea-serpent handles are fantasies compensated for by the simplicity of the reed and tie rims, the mobile yet orderly border to the domed cover and the simple swell of the body. The arms are those of Philip Yorke, who was created Baron Hardwicke in 1733. ▼

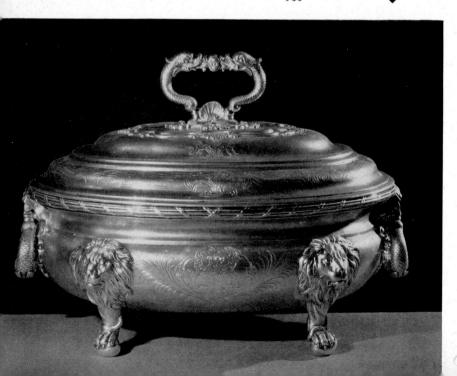

▲ PLATE 75

A small coffee-pot by Charles Kandler which has all the evidence
of Continental inspiration for the English rococo movement. Fluting
is used for a baluster-bodied pot lavishly enriched with scrolls,
shells, foliage, strapwork, trelliswork and matting. The curved spout
is leaf-capped and the base is richly chased with scrolls, a feature
echoed in the sockets for the wood handle.

▶

PLATE 76 In this jug, Paul De Lamerie uses the footed style popular on the
Continent, with pear-shaped body and low-domed cover. The short
spout suggests ribbed sand along the shore, while the foliage and
cast finial contrasts well with the marine fantasy. The jug, $9\frac{1}{2}$ in. high
and weighing 31 oz. 6 dwt., was made in 1738.

PLATE 78

Sober in comparison with the Lamerie jug, this chocolate-pot by Paul Crespin is nonetheless very unusual. Of plain bottle form, with bold handle, the stepped, domed cover has a hinged baluster cover through which the stirring rod is inserted. This is a long and heavy whisk, with six wood flanges at the end, and mounted in silver. To insert it, it is necessary to remove the whole cover. Made in 1738, the pot is inscribed as the gift of the Earl of Dysart to Mrs. Tollemache in 1791, and bears a later coat-of-arms. It is another example of the fine silver in the Farrer Collection at the Ashmolean Museum.

◀

PLATE 77

One of the most remarkable pieces of silver ever made in England is this soup tureen and stand made by Paul Crespin in 1740. Here is rococo sculpture in silver at its most exotic. Models of hinds support an oval vase-shaped bowl which is festooned with cast and chased flowers and foliage. The fluted cover is a riot of grapes, pears, plums and apples, held in place by screws, while citrus fruits are set between the hinds on the oval dish; $21\frac{3}{4}$ in. overall, this piece of magnificence in silver weighs 524 oz.

◀

PLATE 79

Among the pieces commissioned by the Worshipful Company of Goldsmiths to replace plate lost in earlier times was this fine Warwick cruet, one of a pair made for the Company by Richard Bayley in 1740. The vase-shaped casters with their elongated husk and scroll piercing and the elegant, silver-mounted oil and vinegar bottles are typical of the restrained styles that survived even in the high rococo period—a glimpse of which is seen in the decorative scroll and petal feet and the rich shell and foliate encrusted ground for the Company arms which appear in chased relief. ▼

PLATE 80

London silversmiths had an unprecedented mastery of decoration
though sometimes it must be their
virtuosity rather than the silver
that has to be admired. This pair
of sauce boats is by Charles
Kandler, and was made in 1742.
Chased in relief with figures, fish,
birds, animals and of course the
inevitable shells, scrolls and
foliage, the handles formed as
eagles with their prey, the sauce
boats are superb examples of the
high rococo style that was often
akin to porcelain designs which
were popular at this period.

PLATE 82

This two-handled cup and cover,
enriched with gilding, is another
of the commissions ordered by the
Goldsmiths' Company in 1740, this
time from Thomas Farren. Standing 15¼ in. high, the cup is a fine
example of English rococo. On one
side is chased a figure of Minerva
amid scrolls and flowers, on the
other the Company's arms. Masks,
scrolls, foliage and fruit cluster
around the cover, which is topped
by a pineapple finial, said to be
the emblem of hospitality. The
asymmetry of the rococo is further
emphasised by the different terms
to the handles, one a satyr's head,
the other a Bacchante. ▼

PLATE 81

Even apparently simply designed
silver did not quite escape the
influence of the rococo. This
large circular salver, with its
shaped moulded rim and orderly
arrangement of scrolls and shell
motifs, merely hints at the rococo,
though the engraved coat-of-arms
at once betrays the full influence
of the style, with its elaborate
asymmetrical cartouche. The salver, 14 in. in diameter, and weighing 51 oz., was made in 1744 by
Robert Abercrombie, a silversmith who largely specialised in
the skilled work of making trays.

◀

PLATE 83

Candlesticks were an ideal subject for the rococoists, since the ornament could hardly interfere with function. This candlestick from a set of four, is cast and chased in high relief with three dolphins between three different masks set amid scrolls and wave-like motifs which rise to the shell-encrusted chased and matted baluster stem. Swirled fluting, foliage and scrolls decorate the sconce. The detail of the cast chasing can perhaps best be appreciated with the information that the candlestick is only $9\frac{1}{2}$ in. high. Made by John Jacob in 1740 it is now in the Farrer Collection, Ashmolean Museum, Oxford.

PLATE 84

Nicholas Sprimont was a silversmith who in 1749 became the manager
of the Chelsea Porcelain factory. His feeling for the rococo was,
even in silver, almost that of the potter. This deep oval cake basket,
made in 1745, in fact shows a detail very akin to English porcelain
patterns. It stands on bold cast and pierced scroll feet with shell
knuckles, and finely modelled heads rise from naturalistic wheat-
sheaf sprays at either end. The wheat theme is repeated along the
handle, which rises from finely modelled flowers and foliage, while
the sides are a trelliswork of engraved lattices and flowerhead motifs.

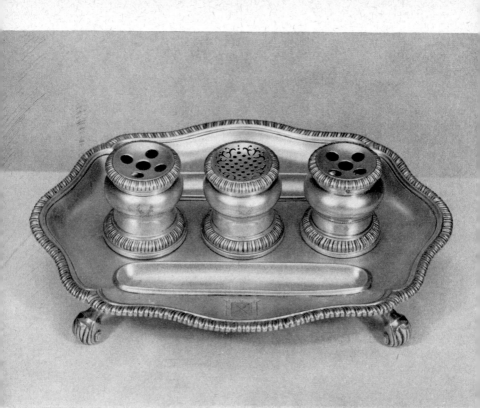

▲ PLATE 85

This inkstand, on four scroll feet
shows the mid-eighteenth century
liking for a shaped stand, but
retains the formal gadrooned
borders of the baroque period.
There is a shallow well on either
side of the three vase-shaped pots
for ink and pounce. One pot is
later, dated 1804, perhaps a re-
placement for a lost bell or
another sand-box; $11\frac{1}{2}$ in. wide,
the stand weighs 44 oz. 17 dwt.
Made in 1747 by William Cripps.

PLATE 86

Here William Cripps interprets
the rococo by suggestion rather
than letting it dominate his design.
The circular bases, with a formal
border of guilloches, are charmingly applied with swirling foliage. The stems, rising from scrolls,
are chased with husks that swell
into leaf-bordered scrolls enclosing scalework, asymmetrical
yet orderly. Formality also typifies
the simple borders for the sconces.
Made in 1747, they weigh 46 oz.

▶

PLATE 88

Here Paul De Lamerie uses the pedestal style for a pair of circular salts of 1748, each on a spreading moulded foot with knopped section above and applied palm leaves at the base of the circular bowl.

▼

PLATE 87

Columns formed as caryatids have been favoured by architects from earliest times, and the idea has been long repeated by the silver-smith. Classical draped figures, such as those created by Anthony Nelme in 1694, now in the Bank of England collection, kneeling slave boys, such as those by John Pero, 1733, formerly in the Harewood collection, and here, a male and a female caryatid translated into the rococo style trace their changing history in English silver. This pair, by Paul De Lamerie, was made in 1748, near the end of his life. An identical pair of 1752 by Frederick Kandler was apparently cast from the same moulds, Kandler pre-sumably having bought some of Lamerie's tools at auction after the latter died in 1751.

PLATE 89

Dining-table silver of the mid-eighteenth century was usually sturdy. These two sauce boats, made by Daniel Piers in 1749, together weigh 27 oz. 4 dwt. The unusual "quilted" decoration on the feet and double-scroll handles is one that appears to have been introduced from the Continent at a time when many patrons were beginning to tire of the meander-ings of the rococo; it was even on occasions used for candlestick stems and for the bodies of tureens. On these sauce boats, the asymmetry of the engraved coats-of-arms in their rococo cartouches contrasts with the formal sim-plicity of the gadrooned borders. ▼

PLATE 90

A fine cup and cover of 1753 that could well have been made thirty
years earlier. Its formal applied strapwork at the base of the body
and on the domed cover, the leaf-capped, double-scroll handles,
and the moulded rib about the lower part of the body betoken the
still-abiding influence of the early Huguenot period. The engraved
coat-of-arms and its flowing rococo cartouche indicate the later
date of the engraving, which is, in fact, also confirmed by the hallmark
for 1753 and the maker's mark—that of John Swift.

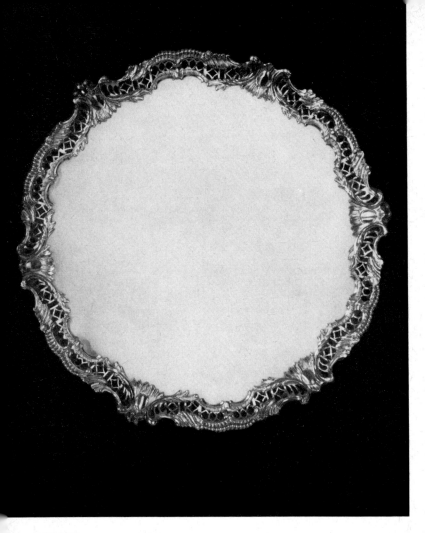

PLATE 91

A touch of the chinoiserie inspires the pierced frets on the border
of this beautiful salver made by Edward Aldridge and John Stamper
in 1758. Around the pierced gallery, the border is shaped with
gadroons, shells and scrollwork in finely cast and chased work that
contrasts sharply with the absolute plainness of the centre. Weighing
51 oz. 8 dwt., the salver is $13\frac{7}{8}$ in. in diameter.

PLATE 93

Throughout the eighteenth century, the tea-table retained its position as the centre of conversation in society. Literature of the period is full of tea-drinkings, and no well-appointed drawing room was complete without tea-table silver. Tea caddies, often made en suite with sugar bowls, became box-like or bowl-like, instead of following the bottle-topped canister styles of the early years of the century. A specialist maker of caddies was Samuel Taylor, who made this rococo caddy of circular form, repoussé chased with asymmetrical scrolls and bold festoons of different fruits and flowers, in 1759. 6 in. high, it weighs just 10 oz.

◀

PLATE 92

Specialist makers often concentrated on certain groups of silver and supplied the trade with wares such as salvers, salts, casters and even épergnes. One of the noted makers of casters was Samuel Wood of Gutter Lane, and even within the limitations of the vase shape, he managed to achieve variations so that it is often difficult to find a pair or a trio alike. Here three matching casters of 1755 have the domed covers pierced with spiral fluting and foliage, one of the smaller pair being less openly pierced, presumably for use as a pepper caster. The tallest is just under 8 in. high.

PLATE 94 Bold, weighty and simple—the keynotes of many fine baluster-shaped jugs, probably mostly used for beer throughout the eighteenth century. Indeed, many are inscribed with labels such as "Small" and "Strong", or with the initials "A" and "B" for ale and beer. This sturdy jug, weighing 52 oz. 17 dwt., has typical moulded circular foot, baluster-shaped body with moulded rim and short spout relying for its decoration on the leaf-capped scroll handle and the shell motif applied below the lip. By Shaw and Priest, 1758. ▼

1760–1800

"A complete set of very beautiful white and gold china for tea, and a coffee pot, tea pot, cream jug and milk jug in silver, in forms remarkably pretty."

Fanny Burney's record of a New Year
gift from the Queen: January, 1787

Simplicity, even severity, was a natural reaction from the rococo, and in every branch of art and architecture the new classicism found ready adherents, though by no means all approved of Adam's particular style. The beginning of the young George III's reign in 1760 was a turning-point in the social history of Britain. Industry was having prodigious and hideous effects on the towns; machines were being developed, new techniques perfected to produce wares at twice the speed and half the price of the hand-made product. The machine was not a thing to be decried, but a subject for marvel. And for the first time, English designers developed new ideas themselves, leading the way with their application of the new classicism. From 1762 onwards, Matthew Boulton had great success with silverware and Sheffield Plate made at his Soho factory in Birmingham; the simpler styles introduced by Adam were very suited to his new methods and to those of the Sheffield makers. In London the silversmiths remained chiefly hand-craftsmen, but were, of course, in the forefront with the new classicism, and when others besides Horace Walpole began to complain of Adam's "gingerbread, filigraine and fan-painting", they conceived richer, but still formally classical and graceful styles for their silver tureens and teapots, vases, jugs, dishes and baskets.

PLATE 95 ▶

The tall, baluster-shaped coffee-pot on a circular foot came into fashion round about 1755. The cover of these new-style pots became rather more domed, while the curved spout was often decorated with scroll, leaf or even fantastic ornament, an eye-like motif often appearing above the beak of the spout. Acorn or flame finials were popular, as on this coffee-pot by Jacob Marsh, which is dated 1768. The pot $10\frac{3}{8}$ in. high, weighs 27 oz., and features applied leafage on the spout and scroll decoration at the socket of the wood handle.

PLATE 96

The 1760's were especially notable years for the centrepiece or épergne. A noted maker of épergnes was the immigrant Norwegian, Emick Romer, while Thomas Pitts, who was recorded in Air Street, Piccadilly, from 1767 until 1793, supplied nothing but épergnes to the distinguished firm of Parker and Wakelin. This elaborate example by Pitts, made in 1763, its base a lattice of scrolls and foliage rising to a lacy stem and oval basket, also features four sets of candle branches. 13 in. high, it weighs 206 oz. 3 dwt.

PLATE 98 ▶

One of the delights of English silver is the tumbler cup, a small base-heavy cup that returns to upright if tipped. They were made in large numbers, both in London and the Provinces, from the end of the Charles II period onward, and, apart from an inscription, initials or a crest, most are usually quite plain. This pair, engraved elaborately with a coat-of-arms in a floral and foliate cartouche, are relatively late examples (1767). Each is 2½ in. high and weighs 3 oz. 10 dwt. They were made by Thomas Whipham & Charles Wright.

PLATE 97 ▲

More austere, a trio of caddies and a sugar box by Albert Shurman, made one year later in 1764. Of rectangular form, each side is engraved with borders of flowers and foliage. Narrow gadroons edge the shallow-domed covers, which have similar borders of flowers around the engraved arms of Vansittart impaling Morse on the top of each. Each of the two caddies is $2\frac{3}{4}$ in. wide, the sugar box is $3\frac{1}{4}$ in. wide, and the three weigh together 43 oz. 13 dwt.

PLATE 99

The 1760's were years of somewhat indecisive style in English silver. People were tired of asymmetry. Some designers turned to France for new inspiration, some attempted to modify the rococo, others looked further back to the rich dignity of the baroque. Here Ebenezer Coker harnesses the motifs of the rococo for a candlestick from a set of eight made in 1768; 11 in. high, fluted stems rise from shaped shell-chased bases; the shoulders are chased with formal shell motifs, and the borders gadrooned. The eight sticks together weigh 183 oz. 10 dwt.

PLATE 100

French styles at the period were already formal, and in this candlestick from a set of four, made in 1767 and 1771, William Cripps offers his version of the French formality. The circular base is chased with a border of foliage, and is otherwise plain except for the owner's arms. A knop of reed and ribbon design acts as a base for the tapered, fluted stem which is also fluted at the shoulder and from which rise the palm-leaf chased sockets; 9 in. high, the four candlesticks weigh 93 oz. 3 dwt.

PLATE 101

Hints of a return to the baroque are seen in this square-based candlestick made by John Romer in 1771. Standing 12 in. high, and weighing 46 oz., it has a boldly gadrooned base and socket, and a gadrooned border to the detachable sconce. The leaf-chased and fluted stem rises from a plain well, the tapered fluting giving it an elegantly slender appearance.

PLATE 102

The impact of the young Robert Adam on architecture and interior design was far-reaching. This neo-classical candlestick, from a pair now in Temple Newsam, Leeds, was made by John Carter in 1767 to a design actually in the Adam drawings in the Soane Collection. Detailed acanthus-leaf borders and a circle of guilloche ornament decorate the base; then acanthus chasing rises to slender flutes, which in turn support a baluster stem of foliage chasing and spiral fluting. Palm leafage above, favoured by the neo-classicists, spreads out to the shoulder; the sockets are rich with palm and acanthus leaves.

PLATE 103

One of the delights of English silver is that so often there is a gentle sense of humour, even of satire, in the decoration. In the late seventeenth century, chinoiseries had a simple smiling aspect. Half a century later, in 1723, the engraver of the Treby punch bowl, probably Hogarth, peopled the sides for the maker, Paul De Lamerie. In the 1750's, chinoiseries returned in a new guise—flowery and rococo. After the rococo, the sense of humour remained—as in this set of pierced caddies and sugar box, with blue glass liners gleaming through scenes pierced on the rectangular sides, and with other figures perched as finials on the foliate covers. By William Vincent, 1771.

PLATE 104

The advantage of the rococo from the craftsman's point of view was that it called for all his skills—casting, repoussé chasing, matting, piercing, modelling. Here Vincent reveals how delicate applied work and pierced detail give lightness and even a fragile look to silver. The caddies are of shaped oblong form, on flower-chased feet, and are overlaid with applied chased trails of flowers and foliage, a theme repeated for the pierced sugar basket with its rose-mounted cover and corded and chased swing handle. The set was made in 1769.

PLATE 105

Beading was less common on cutlery and flatware than feather-edge with a slanted cut flute, or the plain Old English pattern with flat stem and rounded end that dominated tableware designs from the mid-eighteenth century onwards, and which is still made. Matched sets of cutlery and flatware are very rare, and most sets are often deficient in the number of forks and almost always of knives. This set with beaded borders dates between 1775 and 1781.

PLATE 106

Simple even to a point of plainness, a gravy pot and stand by Charles Aldridge and Henry Green. Often known as argyles, these gravy pots were most necessary vessels in days when kitchens were often far from the dining saloon. An inner section held hot water or a heated billet, keeping the gravy warm. Handles were often insulated with wicker. Strainer holes for the spout were, curiously, often very small indeed. This plain beaded pot was made in 1777, its stand three years later. ▼

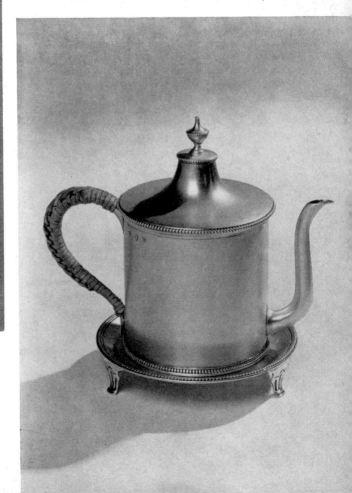

PLATE 107

Silver by the Bateman Family has won for itself a special place among collectors, very largely because of the glamour associated with a woman's running a silver business. Hester Bateman was no doubt a very hard-headed businesswoman, a trait apparent also in her daughter-in-law, Ann, who registered her mark with Peter Bateman in 1791. Just before then, in 1790, the rarest of all the Bateman marks was registered—that of Peter and his brother Jonathan. This teapot, typical of its date, with its panels edged with bright-cut engraving, its draped and festooned engraved cartouche, oval, domed cover and straight spout, was made by Peter and Jonathan Bateman in 1790.

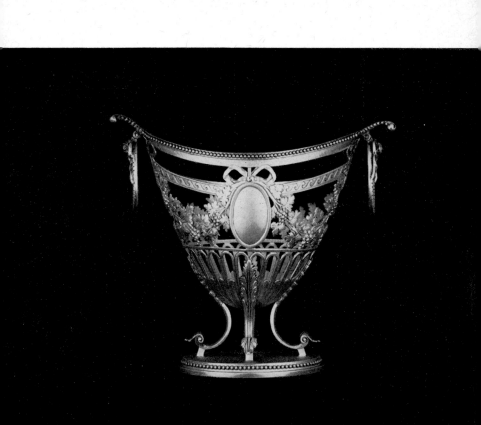

PLATE 108

Not all Adam period silver was plain, though much owed something
to classical inspiration, despite the fact that few pieces of classical
metalwork were known. Vase and boat shapes dominated form,
sometimes charmingly pierced out to take blue glass liners—as with
this delicate sugar basket made by Robert Hennell in 1782. Beading,
vine festoons, a beribboned oval plaque and ring handles are marks
of neo-classicism, while the form echoes a classical footed stand.
The basket is 6¼ in. high. Robert Hennell, who completed his apprenticeship in 1763, was one of a long- and still-working family of
silversmiths. In 1773 he set up on his own account as a saltmaker.

▲ PLATE 109

Two London silversmiths who seem to have specialised in the very particular craft of making trays were John Crouch and Thomas Hannam. Many trays were very large—up to 40 in. wide—and comparably heavy, perhaps 320 or even 340 oz. Simple reeded or beaded borders with matching handles sheathed in leafage were almost standard, though a fluted inner border was also a favourite style. The tray shown is 23 in. wide, weighs 118 oz. 16 dwt., and was made by Hannam and Crouch in 1793.

PLATE 111

This sauce tureen of 1795 shows all the characteristics of the "oval" period. On an oval reeded foot, and with reeded loop handles accentuating the oval form of the body, the tureen is delicately engraved with bright-cut foliage below the reeded rims, and with bright-cut panels on either end. The tureen is one of a pair which weigh 36 oz. 14 dwt.; they were made by John Robins.

▶

PLATE 110 ▲

This circular vegetable dish made by Paul Storr, in 1794 shows the silversmith's mastery of chasing and his innate liking for simplicity of line. The plain bodies have drop handles, and have reed-and-tie rims. The covers, chased with radiating palm leafage, have reeded handles, and are engraved with armorials. The dish is one of a set of four, together weighing 127 oz. 16 dwt.

PLATE 112

The years at the turn of the century were very much years of invention, innovation, and gadgets for the table. Methods of making coffee and keeping it hot occupied the time of various inventors, including one, called Biggin, who invented a percolator. A number were made in silver, and were accompanied by a stand and lamp. This early example, made by John Emes in 1797 shows the typical short-spouted cylindrical pot, here charmingly engraved with bright-cut festoons. The lamp and stand, with reeded paw feet, are, however, later, and were made in 1821, by another maker, possibly William Sumner.

PLATE 113 ▲

The growing taste for decorative plate did not entirely dominate the early years of the nineteenth century, and for less opulent patrons, the silversmiths still made much in the Adam style. This set of four pedestal salts of 1803, each on a plain-moulded foot and with gadrooned everted rims, is typical of the simple, functional silver still being made. The maker was perhaps Robert Salmon.

PLATE 114

The more traditional type of standish or inkstand formed as a rectangular tray with depressions for pens and containers for ink and sand never lost its popularity. Here the stand has a gadrooned border and panel feet, while the now almost standard glass with silver mounts is used for the bottles. It bears the arms of Francis Godolphin Osborne, 5th Duke of Leeds; made in 1798 by William Simmonds, it weighs 37 oz. 1 dwt. ▼

PLATE 115

A charming form of inkstand, apparently the design of John Robins whose mark appears on most recorded examples of this type, is the globe inkstand. This one dates from 1801, and stands on a circular reeded foot, the frame decorated with shells and with a leaf finial. There is a small block inside to hold the ink bottles, which are always of glass mounted in silver, and to contain the pens. ▶

1800–1830

"One of Rundell and Bridge's beautiful silver girandoles came too near the curtain which immediately blazed up."

Prince Puckler-Muskau: *A Regency Visitor*,
1826–8

Though the Regency itself lasted only from 1811 until 1820, the style preceded and outlasted those nine years, and covers in fact the thirty years of the commanding influence of George, both as Prince of Wales, Regent and King. It was a style born of Adam, and a natural development of his most restrained classicism. The war with France did not prevent French ideas from sweeping through London, and indeed actually encouraged them; furniture was enriched with ormolu and other mounts, though much less extensively than in France at the period. Henry Holland provided houses and furniture with majestic proportions, Thomas Hope and George Smith both created furniture designs interpreting Greek, Roman and Egyptian styles, and when demand for something yet different faced the designers, they turned once more to China and the East. The diversity of Regency design was perhaps to some extent the responsibility of the Prince, who veered from one style to another as he began to appreciate the finer details of each new idea. The taste for grandeur was, however, almost universal, and the Royal goldsmiths – Rundell, Bridge and Rundell – found "the Nobility and Gentry . . . anxious to vie with each other in every species of luxury and Extravagance, and such orders were given by them for splendid services of Plate and costly suits of Jewels as has not been before thought of". Prince, peer and commoner alike made life in the 1820's "busy and profitable" not only for Rundell & Bridge but for all the silversmiths, and for all those catering for that great new market which was prepared to buy less grand silver or even substitutes provided they looked like silver.

PLATE 116 Here Daniel Smith and Robert Sharp apply finely modelled heads of Perseus within the intertwined chased serpent handles of a wine cooler, one of a pair made by them for the leading jewellers, Rundell, Bridge & Rundell in 1804. The band around the top of the vase-shaped bodies encloses medallions within dolphin cartouches of the arts and sciences, and coats-of-arms in draped cartouches. 10¼ in. high, the two coolers weigh 248 oz. 8 dwt.

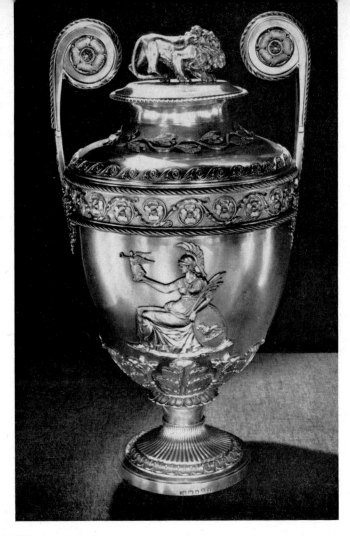

PLATE 117

Victory against Napoleon at sea was a challenge to the navy. For the silversmith, the challenge lay in creating sculpture in silver to John Flaxman's design for the Trafalgar Vases. Sixty-six of these vases were awarded to sea commanders. A large number of these were made by one of the most skilled silversmiths of the period, Benjamin Smith. Most approximate to the design is this one, made in 1808, with an applied figure of Britannia on one side, acanthus and acorn chasing round the base of the body, corded scroll handles with rosette centres and boldly modelled lion finial above.

PLATE 118

Plate issued to British Ambassadors was appropriately lavish, and
on their retirement most ambassadors retained the plate as a per-
quisite of office. In 1814, the Duke of Wellington was appointed
ambassador in Paris, and took with him a fine array of plate, including
this silver-gilt sugar vase and cover, now in the collection at Apsley
House, London. Dated 1810, and measuring 8 in. high, it is richly
chased with palmettes and foliage of classical inspiration. It was one
of the standard designs made by Digby Scott and Benjamin Smith
who produced them from about 1803 onwards.

PLATE 119

Probably of all Regency period
silversmiths, the name of Paul
Storr is best known. He, too,
spent many years working for
Rundell, Bridge & Rundell, and
executed many magnificent pieces
of silver for them. This candle-
labrum, made in 1814, one of a
pair weighing together 522 oz.,
stands 37 in. high. Executed in
silver gilt the lights are supported
on scrolling, reeded branches
rising from the central, plain-
fluted column, the base of which is
a sculptured scene with cast
chased models of Pan playing his
pipes surrounded by nymphs and
goats.

PLATE 120

Much important Regency period
silver was gilt. This set of four
decanter stands by William Bur-
wash, made in 1817, shows the
restrained magnificence of the best
of Regency plate. The hooped
wire sides are overlaid with grapes
and wine-leaf motifs, realistically
chased and rising from a plain
gadrooned rim. The centres are
engraved with crests below coro-
nets. Each is 6 in. in diameter,
with a wood base.

PLATE 121

Just as Wedgwood spent painstaking years
perfecting copies of the Portland Vase,
so the silversmiths essayed the marble
Warwick Vase in silver, casting and chasing
the applied classical figures with patience
and skill. Having achieved replicas, the
silversmiths adapted the vase for ice pails,
tureens and centrepieces, and Storr was
among the foremost of the copyists. When
Storr broke with Rundell, Bridge & Rundell, the firm continued to make Warwick
Vases, among them this replica, one of a
pair made in 1819 by Philip Rundell.
Engraved with the monogram of Harriet,
Duchess of St. Albans, it is $9\frac{3}{4}$ in. high.
The pair weighs 333 oz.

PLATE 122

Most of the Rundell, Bridge and Rundell
production of the 1820's was based on the
designs carried out by Storr and others
during the last years of George III. This
large soup tureen with half-fluted body,
shaped gadrooned and shell border, and
reeded and leaf-decorated handles, weighs
107 oz. 15 dwt. It shows a nice balance between the richness of ornament and the
dignity of plain surfaces. It was made by
Philip Rundell in 1820.

PLATE 123

This oval silver-gilt cake basket was made in 1820 by J. & E. Terry. On four shell and scroll feet, with broad, everted rim, pierced and chased with horses and hounds amid swags of fruit and flowers, it shows the early nineteenth-century interpretation of the rococo— rather more formal and flowery than that of the middle years of the previous century. There are, however, still touches of humour in the dolphin terminals to the flower-chased swing handle. ▼

PLATE 124

This columnar inkstand is dated 1821, and was possibly a gift from George IV to the Marchioness Conyngham or her husband. Three small inkwells, each covered with a Royal crown, are placed on the triangular plinth between cast chased figures of Homer, Virgil and Milton, while a winged Victory surmounts the palm-tree column. This massive piece of silver-gilt stands $28\frac{1}{2}$ in. high, and weighs 230 oz. 5 dwt. It bears the mark of Philip Rundell. ▶

PLATE 125

Tea-table silver, if less impressive than that for the dining room, was nonetheless elaborated with ornament in high relief during the 1820's, and was on occasions also gilded—as this five-piece set made in 1822 and 1823 by William Eaton. It is in the popular melon shape with fluted and panelled bodies chased with flowers and foliage, and with rose finials to the hot-water jug, teapot and hot milk jug. Note the unusually large size of both sugar bowl and cream jug. The gross weight of the set is 112 oz. 3 dwt.

PLATE 126

When Paul Storr left Rundell, Bridge &
Rundell, apparently in 1819, he opened his
own workshops in Clerkenwell, and remained in business until five years before
his death in 1844. Among his last works
must have been this well-shaped dessert
dish from a set of four made in 1838,
formerly in the Tollemache Collection.
Cast and chased models of tritons blowing
conches appear to pull the shell dish
along over a rocky base—a single dish
weighs over 102 oz. It shows Storr's
superb mastery of modelling and of
fluidity of form.

1830–1900

"The growth and development of artistic design, and the appreciation and preference shown it by the advancing taste of the public is strongly exemplified in the works of taste and elegance manufactured . . ."

Watchmaker, *Jeweller* & *Silversmith* journal, 1888

The Victorians were nothing if not confident. Architects and painters, sculptors and artists in stained glass were quite unconcerned if asked to design for another medium than their own. On the other hand, the manufacturers were quite happy that their remorseless search for novelty was the proper development of style. In the reign of William IV and during the early part of Victoria's reign, the richly ornamented rococoism of late Regency remained the chief influence on silver design. Some of the artist-craftsmen did their best to diverge from this, and, led by Pugin, they revelled in a Gothic revival. But the manufacturers trod their own paths, and a group of pieces shown by Elkington & Co. at the Great Exhibition of 1851 were chosen because they were "partly of original design and partly adapted copies from the antique". The result, if very much contrary to present-day taste, was nonetheless skilfully executed, though in less workmanlike hands such highly decorated silver tended to be flimsy and unfunctional. An effort to remedy this was made by Alfred Stevens, a painter and designer who worked for one of the Sheffield silversmiths, Thomas Bradbury, and by Dr. Christopher Dresser, a far from orthodox designer who anticipated cubism in his teapot and other designs for James Dixon & Sons. Towards the end of the century, the split between craftsman and factory was broadened with the arts and crafts movements – such as the Guild of Handicraft, which created *art nouveau* and fostered the academic approach to design. For the factories, silver design tended to consist in reproducing old models or interchanging parts to assemble 'new' ones. It was, perhaps, small wonder that the collecting of antique silver began to become a fashionable pursuit for those who admired the metal.

PLATE 127

A firm prominent in nineteenth-century London silversmithing circles was Garrard's, and here Robert Garrard proves himself an exponent of good Victorian design in a large rosewater dish, 16¼ in. in diameter, from a set of six made in 1851 for the Worshipful Company of Goldsmiths. There is an unexpected dignity in the shell and scroll chasing and the shaped gadrooned rim, while the Company's arms in relief harken back to the elegance of the 1740's.

PLATE 129

The rococo influence survived into the last quarter of the nineteenth century, though often in a more restrained and formal manner than before. This fine cruet stand, with scroll-pierced sides, cast scroll feet and shell central handle holds six blue glass bottles for condiments and sauces. It was made by Robert Harper in 1874.

▶

PLATE 128

Inheritors of a long tradition were the firm of Edward Barnard & Sons, who could trace their history back to the Nelmes in the early 1700's. This fine large inkstand, on four bold scroll feet, was made in 1856. In an age of steel pens and blotting paper, most of the accoutrements of the traditional inkstand remain, even to a sand caster, now of cut glass mounted with silver. A charming feature is the taperstick with cast chased dolphin handle.

▼

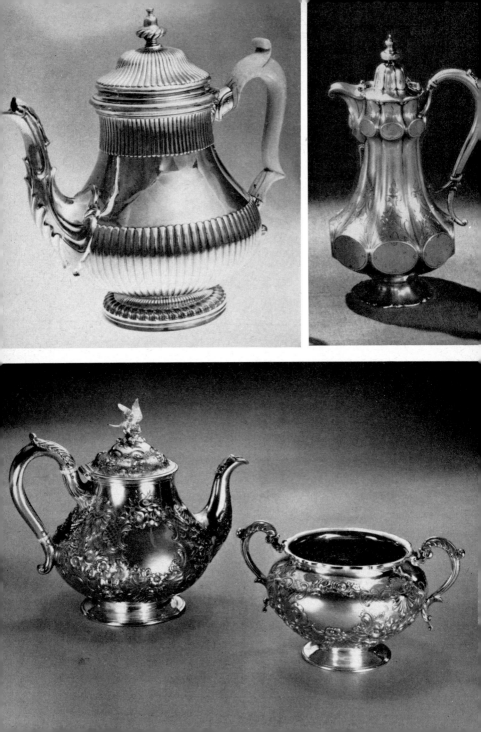

PLATE 130

Efforts to improve design standards were legion during the Victorian
period, and while few silversmiths could resist the lure of adding
decoration, some silver was relatively simple. Even the Gothic
Revival of the middle part of the century did not entirely overwhelm
domestic silver, though ceremonial silver was certainly much
more elaborate. This hot-water jug with strapwork decoration above
the ovals was part of a tea service of 1853. The half-fluted coffee
pot dates from 1861, and is of the same basic form as the much chased
pot and sugar bowl of 1858. This is a good example of the scroll
and flower style of the period, a style not infrequently applied
to earlier plain silver by the so-called "improvers".

PLATE 131

About 1900, the idea of craft
guilds, whose members specialised
in hand-made wares, was firmly
established. Though the aim of
men, such as C. R. Ashbee, was to
improve the standards of design
and craftsmanship, the result was
a deeper chasm than ever between
the craftsman and the large-scale
manufacturer. The craft silversmiths used heavy gauge silver,
and their chief inspiration lay in
the Middle Ages, leavened with a
touch of Art Nouveau. This mus-
tard-pot with green glass liner
combines pierced, chased and
punched work, has a coloured
gemstone set in the finial and was
made by the Guild of Handicraft
about 1900. ▶

THE TWENTIETH CENTURY

"Respect for the past does not mean neglect for the future."
The Worshipful Company of Goldsmiths, 1961

The legacy of Victorian factories and guilds of craftsmen was a divorce of that marriage of art with industry so much desired but so rarely accomplished in the nineteenth century. Ever since then, designers and craftsmen have been endeavouring to establish their proper place in industry, and now, more than halfway through the twentieth century, their goal is well in sight, and is often indeed achieved. Silversmithing, still the most traditional and conservative of the applied arts, is slowly finding modern expression in the face of public shyness of cleaning and of competition from a host of new materials. Two world wars, with their wastage of skills and youth, have had much the same effect as the Civil War of three hundred years ago. Only now are the young men returning to the craft, and finding patrons to sponsor them. The patrons are new – companies and corporations rather than individual members of the public – but the skills are old. There is less retrospection, except to learn the craft. The young designers are striving to express themselves in new terms, creating subtle curves and boldly simple lines that suit the lustre of silver – neither slavishly copying the past nor innovating for the sake of novelty. Though simplicity is the keynote of most modern silver design, the silversmiths of today are not afraid of using detail – cast, chased, engraved or pierced; they may use traditional materials such as ivory, or they may turn to new ones such as nylon for finials and handles; sometimes they have to find new shapes for new wares – for pepper mills and cigarette boxes, for maces and ceremonial cups that reflect not only a famous past but a changing present.

PLATE 132

Trained with a firm of manufacturing silversmiths, Gilbert Leigh Marks prided himself on his hand-craftsmanship and held a number of exhibitions of his work in London. This two-handled cup is embossed and chased with apples and leafage. Standing just over $10\frac{3}{4}$ in. high, it is $8\frac{3}{4}$ in. in diameter, and was made by Marks in 1901.

PLATE 134

Reminiscent of traditional styles, this beaker with its engraved mermaid motif was designed in 1929 by Professor R. M. Y. Gleadowe and made the same year by A. G. Murphy.

◀

PLATE 133

An architect who turned to metalwork, Henry Wilson was for many years an instructor at the London Central School of Arts and Crafts, and President of the Arts and Crafts Exhibition Society from 1915 to 1922. His own work extended in many directions—from furniture and wallpaper designs to fireplaces. Here he used chasing, casting and applied decoration for a large chafing-dish and stand, made in silver with gold mounts, about 1906. He died in the late 1920's.

PLATE 135

A pepper and salt set, made in 1947 for Sir Alan Barlow who gave it to Corpus Christi, Cambridge, to commemorate his election as Fellow in 1946. The stems are formed as a pelican in her piety—taken from the College arms. The salts are gilt inside, and the bases are ornamented with a row of fox heads, a punning reference to Bishop Foxe (founder of the College). More amusing symbolism is suggested by owls (for Bishop Oldham) on the covers of pepper-pots and salt spoons. The smaller salts are $3\frac{3}{4}$ in. high. By Leslie Durbin. ▼

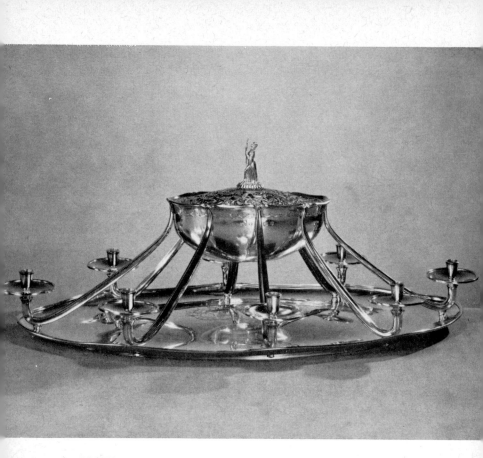

PLATE 136

An elegant candelabrum of eight lights which won an open competition organised by the Goldsmiths' Company. It was designed by Eric G. Clements and made by Mappin and Webb, Ltd. in 1953.

PLATE 137

This sugar dredger is one of a pair presented by Mr. Roy Wilkinson, Mayor of Nuneaton, to Nuneaton Corporation in celebration of its fiftieth anniversary of the granting of its charter. The height of the dredger is $7\frac{1}{4}$ in. It was designed by R. G. Baxendale and made in 1958 by the firm, Wakely & Wheeler Ltd.

PLATE 139 ▶

This very fine gilt-lined water jug was made in 1963 for Exeter College. The designer was John Donald and the maker Tony Lewis.

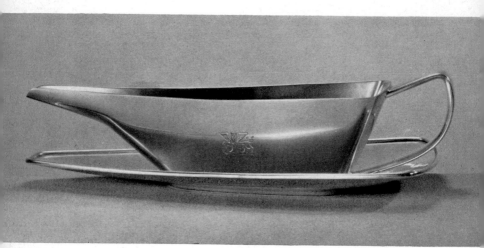

▲ PLATE 138

This elegant sauce boat and stand is part of a dinner service which was made for the Ionian Bank, London, by Gerald Benney in 1960.

PLATE 140

A Loving Cup presented to Sir Frederick Hoare, lately Lord Mayor, by the Worshipful Company of Goldsmiths on behalf of the City of London. The coats-of-arms are those of the City, Sir Frederick, and the Goldsmiths' Company. The cup was designed by Atholl Hill, engraved by T. C. F. Wise and made in 1963 by Wakely & Wheeler Ltd.

◀

INDEX

Plate numbers are in **bold face**